Click, Click, Who's There?

Written by Koh

~

About The Author

Koh's background as both an educator and technology specialist brings a unique perspective to her readers. Since her first love was the classroom, her viewpoint about technology comes from an educational and family-oriented foundation.

As a school teacher, Koh has taught in both public and private elementary schools. As a technology training consultant in the 80's, she was heavily involved in the widespread growth of microcomputers in the business world. She united the two areas of specialty by obtaining a graduate degree in Educational Technology.

When Koh became an educational technology specialist, she was constantly approached by parents looking for advice. Her love and concern for families ignited her passion and interest in cyber ethics and cyber safety. Koh has presented papers, facilitated discussions, and provided seminars at conventions such as the National Education Computer Conference, the National Cyber Ethics Conference, and the North Carolina Association of Independent Schools, as well as community colleges, churches, and local groups.

LHK Publishing, LLC
P.O. Box 473312
Charlotte, NC 28247

Copyright © 2004 by Koh

All rights reserved.
This book may not be reproduced in part or whole in any form whatsoever without written permission from the Publisher, with the exception of parts of Chapter 10 and Additional Information: Rules for Safety and Ethics pages, as explicitly stated on those pages.

Printed in the United States of America

ISBN 0-9760294-0-5

With much love

A loving thanks to those who helped me through this process. A special thanks to Maria! To G52 – hugs and kisses for your encouragement and support.   ~Koh

Table of Contents

Introduction:	Before We Begin	1
Chapter 1:	Click, Click, Who's There?	7
Chapter 2:	How Do I Teach Something I Don't Know?	13
Chapter 3:	You Do Not Need To Be an Internet Expert	19
Chapter 4:	What You Do Need To Get Started	21
Chapter 5:	Knowledge Group 1: Know the Source	23
Chapter 6:	Knowledge Group 2: Know the Question	31
Chapter 7:	Knowledge Group 3: Know the Environment	41
Chapter 8:	Making Decisions for Your Family	49
Chapter 9:	Three True Stories	63
Chapter 10:	Your Family's Plan	77

Additional Information:
    Cultivating Criminals?   87
    Rules for Safety and Ethics   95
    List of Resources   101

INTRODUCTION
Before We Begin

In the natural cycle of life, the children of the present day become the next generation of adults. Our children are learning the ethics, tone, and standards to carry into the future. Parents and other adults have always been the main source of guidance for the development of children in their process of becoming tomorrow's adults. For years it has been a matter of passing down culture, heritage, experience, and family beliefs. But now, for the first time in history, parents have been swept away by the hurtling forces of a never-before-seen whirlwind called the internet.

Children need a great deal of help and guidance with ethical and safety issues in a new online world. But today's adults are often unable to provide this guidance because of the whirlwind nature of the internet's arrival. They have no training, background, experience, or history to pass down to their children. Left unequipped, adults are feeling fearful of technology, feeling inadequate in their knowledge, and feeling overwhelmed by the lack of time to "get up to speed." If today's adults cannot guide and lead our children safely and ethically, then what will happen to our children? What will our children bring into the future? What will happen to the moral integrity of tomorrow's society?

Parents need to help guide their children in several areas of this new world of the internet. Three primary areas are ethical behavior, safety precautions, and general usage. Those categories are similar to general child-rearing categories. You teach your child ethics – say thank you, do not lie, cheat, or steal. You teach them safety – look both ways before crossing, do not talk to strangers. You teach them general life skills – how to tie shoes, brush teeth, put toys away.

But teaching those life skills does not pose the same challenge as teaching internet life skills. Technology and the internet have brought a massive, rather intimidating, amount of information, creating a new demand on parents. Where do you begin? Where do you find the time to tackle this enormous challenge?

Introduction – Before We Begin

Purpose

The purpose of this book is to provide you with a family-based approach to help you build a solid foundation for guiding your child in the world of the internet. At the same time, there will be a focus on the ethical considerations of the online world. Since technology is sometimes intimidating and difficult to understand, the information is delivered in a non-technical way, using analogies that are familiar to today's adults.

Once a solid foundation is established, families will feel more secure in their decision-making abilities and may be more likely to welcome technological advice, especially in regard to online safety. Therefore, the second book of this series will use the fundamental framework created to focus on the safety issue. The serious nature of online risks and dangers warrants both a separate book and some technological discussion.

This book will:

~ help alleviate the sense of being overwhelmed by and fearful of technology by understanding that it is perfectly okay if you are not familiar with technology;

~ provide you with the tools you need to guide your child in the online world, with a focus on the ethical issue;

~ use a non-technical, non-threatening approach;

~ give you a hands-on, do it now approach, in a matter of a few hours.

The truth is that you already have all the tools you need. You just need someone to pull it all together for you, in a simple way that does not demand a lot of time.

> The few hours it might take you to go through this book could be one of the greatest investments you will ever make in your family's life.

Introduction – Before We Begin

Who Should Read This Book?

This book was written for everyone. If you answer yes to any one of these questions, then this book was written particularly for you.

~ Do you have children, grandchildren, nieces, nephews, godsons or goddaughters, or any loved ones between the ages of 1-20?

~ Do you plan to have children in the future?

~ Do you sometimes feel afraid of technology?

~ Do you feel that your children know technology better than you do?

~ Do you perhaps avoid the subject of online ethics and safety because you do not really understand it or because it is overwhelming?

~ Do you want to help your children live safely and ethically in the online world but are unsure of what to do?

~ Do you believe in a strong moral and ethical standard for you and your family?

~ Do you wish for society to maintain a strong moral and ethical standard?

~ Do you teach children?

Acknowledging the Technology Industry

Many thanks should be given to the technology industry for bringing about great inventions, medical advancements, and conveniences to our lives. Technology and the companies who have developed it have made a positive impact in countless areas. But even the most positive devices come with possible negative consequences as well.

For example, the automobile is an enormous convenience for traveling, but life-threatening accidents and theft are not uncommon. The airplane is a significant time-saving method of travel, but life-threatening accidents and hijackings do occur. Disease-curing and pain-relieving drugs are, for many, a life-saving invention. But they, too, allow for negative consequences such as serious side-effects or addiction. There are many more examples like firearms, gasoline, and some items as simple as a match or a fan. They all provide benefits but carry possible detrimental effects.

The same holds true for technology. With the positive comes the negative. The existence of these negative effects does not mean technology is bad. It does not mean you should eliminate technology from your life. Automobiles can have negative consequences, but you still use them because you have learned how to drive safely and avoid the dangers. This series of books is intended to help you avoid and minimize the dangers of technology. The intention is not ever to downgrade or discount the value of technology or the technology industry. Use technology and reap the benefits while avoiding the dangers.

Format of the Book

This book is written to you, the reader. It is about us, today's adults. It talks about each child in our society and refers to that child as a "she." Why? The choices were "he" or "she." A coin was flipped. She won. The book refers to your child. The singular "child" is used instead of children, even though many who read this book may have more than one child. Why? Every single child is an individual. Every single child is a key component of the character and composition of our society.

Several chapters mention a parental toolbox. We will be gathering all the knowledge tools we need throughout this book. Put the information in your mental toolbox or keep a written list. At the end of the book, the information will be retrieved, organized, and applied toward a decision-making process for your family. Your toolbox of knowledge may also come in handy for future situations and decisions.

Some of the key points will appear in a box on the page to emphasize the importance and to provide a quick reference in the future. Keep this book handy. Once you have read it, it will be easy to refer back to some of the main points as a refresher and a reminder.

Let's Begin

Chapter 1
Click, Click, Who's There?

When someone knocks at your front door, the whole family hears it, the dog barks, and you can see who it is through the window or a peephole. You can yell out, "Who's there?" and hear the voice of the 12-year-old neighbor or a 40-year-old man. When your child clicks on a mouse, no one, not even your child, hears or sees the millions of strangers on the other side.

Friend or Foe?

The virtual wall of cyber space allows friends and foes to hide behind it. This ability to hide is one of the negative side effects of online communication. Everyone, friend or foe, who communicates online is hidden behind this virtual wall. Some are intentionally hiding, while others are hidden just by design.

Regardless of intent, this shift to online communication is affecting our morals and ethics.

> Our society's morals and ethics are slowly transforming.

The transformation is happening right in front of our eyes, but in such a slow, subtle manner that perhaps you are not fully aware of it. Much like a slow water drip from upstairs, you may not be aware of each drop. But suddenly one day, you look up, and the ceiling is saturated with water. The next day, the ceiling plaster comes crashing down.

Are We Cultivating Criminals?

The internet is changing our society's morals and ethics in the same fashion. Actually, the internet is not doing it. Rather, we are allowing the availability of the internet to change our society's ethical code, standards, and fiber. We are not intentionally creating the change and probably do not even realize it is happening. But it is happening.

We are cultivating the next generation of adults who are learning that they can hide behind a virtual wall and say mean, ugly comments to others. They do not have to consider the feelings of others because they do not have to deal with them face-to-face. They do not have to see or feel anyone's reaction. They are now learning that you can do anything you want on a keyboard and not have to face or deal with the consequences.

The computer is treated like a television. We often scream at the television, during a game, "C'mon ref, what are you, blind?" or a game show, "That's a stupid answer! What were you thinking?" The television is a one-way communication device. Yelling out mean, ugly statements does not hurt anyone's feelings. You are not really directing your curt words to a person who can hear them. You know that, and you also know that you probably would not say those things if you were standing in a room face-to-face with that person. Our children are treating the computer like a television. It is very easy to fall into the mentality of *if I don't see it or have to own up to it, it must not be real.* Yet it is real. A real person is on the receiving end of the computer. A great deal of damage is being done.

We are cultivating the next generation of adults who are learning how easy it is to commit an online crime and how hard it is to get caught. After all, they are just typing on the keyboard in the comfort of their own home. The keyboard is just a typewriter. Today's adults grew up with a typewriter. You click away on a keyboard; what harm can you really be doing? But this typewriter theory does not apply to the internet. It is not just a keyboard, yet it "feels" like it is.

So children (and adults) are sitting at home at the keyboard, sipping on a soda and eating some chips. They do not see the effects and reactions of those who have their identity stolen. They do not see our national security threatened when they tap into the Pentagon's server for the thrill of it. They do not feel the pain of thousands when they play with the stock portfolio of one or several commodities, just to show off to their friends. After all, they were not there to hear the tree fall, so did it really make a sound?

These are not just the few unusual cases. An entire book could be written on examples alone. The number of incidents is so great that the police, FBI, Department of Justice and many agencies have had to develop complete departments to handle such cases. Even the law is struggling to change and keep up-to-date.

This change in ethics is happening slowly and gradually. It is difficult to detect on a day-to-day basis. It is also difficult to detect because morals and ethics are not concrete, measurable objects. On the other hand, the resulting behavior, a crime, is measurable. But by then, the ethical change has occurred. If you are not convinced that such a change is occurring, then refer to "Cultivating Criminals?" located in the Additional Information section at the end of this book. It provides more supporting information.

How It Can Happen: From "You're Ugly" to a Felony

The focus here is not on the crimes themselves. The criminal acts are indeed harmful, sometimes malicious, and need to be punished appropriately. The focus of this first book is that, right now, we are raising and cultivating these criminals. We are allowing our children to learn how to hide behind a virtual wall (the internet) and say (type) mean or ugly messages that they would not normally say face-to-face or on the phone.

A person can easily type "I don't like you," "You're ugly," "No one likes you," or any type of unkind message and not have to deal with the receiver's reaction to this message. The receiver, hurt by these words, decides to "get even" by doing a little simple hacking to get the sender's password and cause some harmless havoc. Then this innocent "nanny nanny poo poo head" behavior grows deeper into, "This hacking stuff is fun. It's so easy. What a thrill! What else can I do?" Suddenly a simple unkind word has grown into a full-blown criminal act. It was never the initial intention to be malicious or to commit a crime. It all started with a "nanny nanny poo poo head."

Chapter 1 – Click, Click, Who's There?

How It Starts: The Tip of the Iceberg

There is no single method of how one becomes an online criminal. No one plans on being a criminal. No one plans to raise a criminal. But it happens. Some of the most damaging crimes (e.g. hacking into the Pentagon, accessing a nuclear plant, manipulating stocks) were committed by teenagers. It is doubtful that these teenagers woke up one morning and decided to be criminals. As a matter of fact, they do not really think they have even committed a crime because they did not hear the tree fall. They simply were typing on their keyboard. They were good kids. They are good kids. Somewhere, somehow, the good kids are being affected. How are good kids being drawn into this behavior? Here is one possible scenario.

The "nanny nanny poo poo head" messages are typed using something as simple as an instant messaging system (IM).[1] It also occurs in email messages. A third avenue is chat rooms. Those are just three examples of online communication devices. All of them are "cold" methods of communication because there is no personal touch, body language, voice intonation, facial expression, or eye contact. The use of emoticons[2] was introduced to help with the coldness of this communication method, but emoticons can be misinterpreted, can be sarcastic, and still allow a user to hide behind the virtual wall. Emoticons cannot replace or express live emotions.

Therefore, despite emoticons or other such emotion-expressing devices, online communication is cold, cold as ice.

---

[1] Instant messaging is compared to being on the telephone, as you can have a "live" conversation with another person. The difference is that it is not truly live. You are online and typing on the "not live" screen. IM will be used as the abbreviation for a generic instant messaging system. The term IM is often associated with a specific vendor, but there are a number of vendors who provide instant messaging software.

[2] An emoticon is a typed series of letters and symbols to represent an emotion. For example: ;-) represents a person winking. There are hundreds of emoticons and abbreviations. An example of an abbreviation is ROFL, rolling on the floor with laughter.

Chapter 1 – Click, Click, Who's There?

> Online methods of communication are as cold as ICE:
>
> I   Instant Messaging
> C   Chat Rooms
> E   Email

Is the seemingly harmless use of ICE developing poor ethical behavior and possibly cultivating criminal behavior? These methods of communication can have benefits, if used properly. What is proper use? Is there a proper use? How does someone learn to use these tools properly?

Friend and Foe

Many families, by now, have heard of the dangers of the internet in terms of safety, pedophiles, and predators. But protecting children and the family while online goes beyond just protecting against intruders. It means protecting their ethical integrity. It means protecting them from being lured into the temptation of criminal activity. Today's online friends are slowly learning foe behavior. The question "Friend or Foe?" is becoming a statement, "Friend and Foe." The task of protecting children online is multi-fold and an enormous responsibility. Parents are responsible for their children, but how do you teach your child about something that you do not know – that did not exist when you were growing up?

CHAPTER 2
How Do I Teach Something I Don't Know?

Much of our parenting skill and wisdom comes from information passed down to us throughout the generations. Our parents taught us everyday manners and safety, but our parents did not teach us about the dangers of the internet or the pitfalls and traps into which we can easily fall. They did not teach us that information because the internet did not exist in the fashion that it does today, basically available to every person in the world.

Nor do you have any personal experience from which to draw. As an adult today, you probably did not grow up with technology or the internet. Therefore, how can you be expected to pass down important safety precautions? Is it your responsibility as a parent to learn everything there is to know about this invention in order to properly teach your child? The answer is, "No."

That is a relief, but parents are still frustrated because some feel that this invention is usurping their authoritative knowledge as a parent. Some feel intimidated by the internet and technology. Some have given in to it, have taken a back seat, and have just let their children become the experts.

The first step is to understand the root of this frustration and confusion. You will see that it is perfectly understandable why so many adults have fallen into this situation. Once you have a healthy perspective and understanding about the big picture, then you will be able to begin to be proactive and take action. Because of the lack of history and wisdom, parents have not been given a chance to develop a strong foundation on which to stand and understand. Here is some information to help you form a stronger foundation.

Chapter 2 – How Do I Teach Something I Don't Know?

Don't Feel Bad – It's Never Happened Before

The exponential growth of the internet is unprecedented and hit our society at such great speeds. Imagine the Wright Brothers' plane in 1903. Now imagine about five years later, in 1908, if there were millions of people flying on thousands of jets across the sky. There would have been no time for rules and regulations to be developed. There would be no Federal Aviation Administration (FAA). There would have been no time for air traffic controllers to be created. Pilots would not be highly trained because there was such a demand for them that schools had to pump them out as fast as they could. Now imagine the accidents, tragedies, and problems that would result.

To drive the point home, imagine if the invention of the automobile "rolled out" just as quickly. Imagine that within a few short years after the invention of the first automobile, millions of cars hit the road. Because of the onslaught of the number of automobiles, no one had time to develop traffic signals, signs, or lanes. There was no time to figure out the need for a driver's license or age requirements, so there are nine-year-olds on the road. There would be no rules or regulations for safety and no Department of Motor Vehicles (DMV). If someone hits you from behind, well, oops, sorry, too bad. There was no time to develop safety devices like seat belts, so when someone hits you from behind, even more oops, sorry, too bad.

Luckily this was not the situation. In our past, most inventions that have had a huge impact on society have been "rolled out" over a period of time. It was a gradual process that allowed for safety, rules, regulations, manners, and agencies to help us get the most benefit with the least danger. Take a breath from that chaotic previous paragraph and compare the past inventions to the internet.

Put It in Perspective: Airplane vs. the Internet

The Wright Brothers are documented for a 1903 success in flying the first "heavier-than-air" craft. It was thirty years later that the first successful passenger flight occurred. Twenty years after that, the first jet flew around the world. At about the same time, the Federal Aviation Administration (FAA) was developed. It took decades before large masses of everyday people flew on a regular basis. Many people today still have never flown on a plane.

The span of the internet's growth to include large masses of everyday people took just a few short years. The true growth of the internet for everyday users began in the early 1990's. Most statistics on "how many internet users" start around 1993 to 1994. After just five to six years (year 2000), it was estimated that there were 327 million users worldwide. In 2004, the estimate is at 729 million users[3]. Some estimate that online traffic will double every year for the next five years.[4]

With such an unprecedented growth, there has been no time to develop an air traffic controller or FAA equivalent for the internet. Would you send yourself or a loved one on a plane trip with 729 million other people in the air without safety rules or control devices? What do you think the ethical environment would be if 729 million people were rushing around to get to their destination with no set guidance, rules, manners, or procedures?

Perhaps those questions seem a bit dramatic or a little drastic. After all, your child is in the safety of your home, able to access the world from the security of your living room. But is she? Could those drastic questions really be an understatement?

> When your child is on the internet, she is running around in a world with 729 million other people.

---

[3]*Global Internet Statistics*, <http://www.glreach.com/globstats/index.php3>. Global Reach, March 2004. Keep in mind most statistics regarding the internet are rough estimates, since there is no way of counting or tracking every user or activity online. There is no central internet headquarters. It is not monitored, policed, or owned by any entity. Statistics are based only on reported cases, and there is no concrete way to measure who has and who has not reported information.

[4] *IDC Research: Worldwide Net Traffic to Rise*, <http://www.nua.ie/surveys/>. NUA Surveys, March 3, 2003.

Chapter 2 – How Do I Teach Something I Don't Know?

On an airplane, you are only in immediate proximity of those around you at that time. On the internet, you have immediate proximity to the other estimated 729 million users. An airplane trip takes anywhere from thirty minutes to many hours. It gives you time to think and reflect. The internet is almost instantaneous, and it takes pride in becoming faster and faster. Millions of children are not getting on and off planes by themselves everyday. Millions of children are not on planes unsupervised everyday.

Many other invention timelines can be examined. But you will find that:

> No other timeline is as intense and profound as the launching and growth of the internet and technology.

The purpose of this section was to help explain why you may be awestruck by the internet and that your anxiety is understandable. One day you were a parent in a world of dolls and toy trucks, and you worried about your child crossing the street or talking to the occasional one-in-a-million stranger. Within a few short years, your child is accessing the whole wide world, and she is amongst millions of strangers. No wonder you feel overwhelmed.

But still, as the parent, you hold the responsibility to teach her proper internet use, especially when it comes to ICE. You might wonder about the role of schools, churches, the government, or other options. This could lead to a philosophical discussion on parenting and the role of the government. But that is not even a topic open for debate at this time. Due to the newness of this invention, all entities are struggling to keep up. The law, schools, agencies, and many individuals are doing an admirable job addressing this issue of safety and ethics. But we are still in the pioneering stage. Perhaps one day, the laws or schools will have an online ethics and safety course requirement much like a driver's education class. But until then, the responsibility falls on the parents.

That may make you feel a little defensive and react, "It's not my fault that I know so little about the internet because it didn't exist when I grew up and because of its rapid infiltration into society." That is true. Today's parents really cannot be blamed for lack of knowledge because of the unprecedented onslaught of this invention. It is as if a violent hurricane is predicted to hit your neighborhood with only a ten-minute notice. The atmospheric conditions occurred at an unprecedented rate with no previous warning or history of such an occurrence. There is not much you could do to prepare for it. Is it your fault that you could not properly prepare?

No, it is not your fault that you have never been faced with a ten-minute warning about a turbulent hurricane. But as the parent, you do what you can to ensure the safety of your family. You use what you know as best you can to do what is needed. You do not just throw your hands in the air and say, "Oh well, let's just give in to this hurricane. This has never happened before, so I do not know what to do. So I'll do nothing." You would not say, "Well if we can't beat 'em, join 'em," and take your whole family outside to face the fierce winds and torrential rain unprotected.

There are two main points here. First, as a parent, you will always resort to your family's safety and ethical foundations to make the best decisions for your family. This will be the topic of a later chapter. Second:

> It does not matter whose fault it is. It does matter who is responsible.

You are responsible. We are responsible. Each person is responsible for his/her own actions, and if you have a child below the age of eighteen, legally you are responsible for that person as well. Also, hopefully, morally, and out of the love in your heart, you are responsible for that person. We cannot use "It's not my fault" as the basis to escape responsibility. "It's not my fault" is not a reason to jeopardize our children. We cannot use "It's not my fault" to allow the face of our ethical culture to change. Yes, it is a huge challenge to be the pioneering parents of this new culture and generation. But you are still the parent.

Chapter 2 – How Do I Teach Something I Don't Know?

It will be helpful when and if an equivalent air traffic control center is developed for the internet. It will be helpful when and if an equivalent FAA or a required safety course is developed for the internet. But until then, as a parent and an adult, you must make the best decisions for you and your family. Now that the issue of fault has been addressed, move away from it and move forward.

If you are responsible for teaching your child about proper internet use, what does that mean? Does it mean you need to start taking internet classes? Does this mean you need to become an internet expert before you allow your child to be online? The answer is: No. How, then, do you teach your child without becoming an expert yourself?

CHAPTER 3
You Do Not Need To Be an Internet Expert

For those of you who are familiar with or try to adhere to the Ten Commandments, the good news is that there has not been an Eleventh Commandment added that says, "Thou shalt be an expert on the internet." Parents are not expected to be an expert in every possible field involved in parenting.

To be a good parent, do you need to have a medical degree with a thorough knowledge about every possible disease or illness? Do you need to have a pharmaceutical degree before administering any drugs to your child? Do you need to be an automotive mechanic and understand every mechanism in an automobile before allowing your child to drive? Do you need to memorize every page in the DMV manual and have expert recall of every highway statistic before allowing your child to get a driver's license? Is it necessary to be a licensed nutritionist before feeding your family? Must you be a certified therapist before talking to your child?

Obviously, no one can be an expert in all areas, and no one is expected to be. The same holds true for the internet. An adult does not have to be an expert on the internet in order to guide a child safely and ethically online. When we teach children to look both ways before crossing, we do not need to know every statistic and probability about pedestrian accidents on the streets. We do not need to memorize and calculate the formula for speed vs. distance of an automobile in relation to speed vs. distance of walking across the road. Still, we are successful in teaching children to look both ways before crossing.

Chapter 3 – *You Do Not Need To Be an Internet Expert*

Likewise, you do not need to be an expert on the internet. You do not need to achieve mastery before allowing your child to be online. If you have been putting off dealing with your child's online behavior or habits because of

- ~ fear of the internet,
- ~ a lack of knowledge,
- ~ time constraints to learn about technology,

then you now know that those reasons do not need to stop you.

You are ready NOW to take action. The following chapters will help you. You only need to invest an hour or two in your life in order to perhaps save your child's life. You only need to invest that small amount of time in order to give your contribution to the transformation of our society's ethical and moral development.

> It is empowering to know that you already have the knowledge and tools that you need and that you can make such a significant positive impact on your child and on society.

Of course, this is not meant to be an excuse not to learn about the internet. As with any area, gaining information and experience will help broaden your foundation and knowledge. You should try to learn as much as you can, as time allows. For now, time has not allowed you to become an expert. So for now, this book will help you get started by organizing the non-technical tools you need to make the best decisions for your family.

CHAPTER 4
What You Do Need To Get Started

You now know that you can let go of the fear of not understanding technology. You do not need technological expertise to help you start making best decisions for your family's online activity. What do you need? You need some non-technical tools, tools you probably already have. What are those non-technical tools? Basic knowledge.

> Arm yourself with basic knowledge.

Chances are great that you already possess this knowledge, but in our busy and hectic lives, it is helpful to have the information presented and organized in a clear, useful manner. This will also make it easier to apply the knowledge toward your decision-making process. The next three chapters will offer information to carry around in your pocket, head, or parenting toolbox. Chapter 8 and Chapter 10 will help you take this information and apply it.

There is an infinite amount of information that would be helpful to know. It could take perhaps an entire volume of encyclopedias to cover all the information. If a volume of encyclopedias was available to you, chances are no one would have the time to read even a small percentage of it. Therefore, here are three, non-technical, key areas that are useful and comprehensive, yet brief enough to tackle realistically.

> The Three Basic Knowledge Groups
>
> Know the Source
> Know the Question
> Know the Environment

CHAPTER 5
Knowledge Group 1: Know the Source

It is comforting to know that you do not have to be an internet expert. It is comforting to know that, because of the unprecedented, exponential growth of the internet, most adults are all in the same boat together. Nonetheless, parents still feel a lot of pressure to have the latest, greatest, and fastest technology. They feel a lot of pressure to learn technology and to keep up with the changes and advancements. They feel pressure to provide their children with the best technological opportunities, so they can grow up to be successful adults. They suffer from related pressures such as:

~ My child knows more than I do. How can I help?

~ I don't really know how many hours a day/week/month my child should be on the computer or online. I fear I may rob her of necessary learning time.

~ I don't really know at what age my child should start using the computer or the internet. I certainly don't want her to get behind and lose out on career opportunities in the future.

~ I have read about the safety issues and tried to place safety boundaries for my child's online usage, but I get this type of response:

> "You're ruining my social life!"
> "Everyone does it."
> "EVERYONE has IM. EVERYONE has email. EVERYONE uses chat rooms."
> "Don't you trust me?"

Chapter 5 – Knowledge Group 1: Know the Source

The Source

Why all this pressure? Who is driving the advancement of technology? Who is driving you to think you must have the greatest, the latest, and the fastest? Who is driving this "need to know – need to have" mentality? Answer: the technology industry. Companies who make money from developing technological tools are the drivers of this catapulting movement.

The technology industry advertises and drives us to feel the "need to know – the need to have" urgency. It drives us to believe we will fall behind the eight ball if we do not keep up. This is their job. Our country's strength and success is based on a capitalistic business premise. The technology industry is earning an A+ in Business 101. If you make widgets, you sell widgets. You advertise them and create a need. You create a demand. The technology industry is doing exactly that.

Now, you as a parent should simply realize and acknowledge the technology industry's motives and efforts. Commend them for a job well done. Commend them for helping the wealth and strength of this country. Thank them for the conveniences they have provided. At the same time, realize that it is not decades of educational research that dictate who, what, or how much technology is needed.

> It is not brain research or human developmental stages that have determined the need to learn technology at certain ages.

Enjoy the benefits, but do not allow yourself to become a victim of the pitfalls. The pitfall, in this case, is allowing yourself to feel pressured or pushed by the "need to know – need to have" momentum. It would be helpful to be able to identify when you are being "pushed" by this momentum. Certain obvious drivers push us, but there are also hidden, subliminal drivers that push us. Here are a few examples to help you start becoming more aware of the hidden drivers.

Chapter 5 – Knowledge Group 1: Know the Source

Hidden Driver Example 1: 45 Million People Can't Be Wrong

Several years ago, there was an article that stated, "45 million people can't be wrong." The article was actually an advertisement for an instant messaging software program. Certainly if 45 million people are using it, why shouldn't you? Those 45 million people are not wrong. There is nothing wrong with using instant messaging (IM). There is something wrong, however, if IM is used inappropriately. There is something wrong if IM is causing an ethical shift in your child's mentality and life behavior. The use of IM or any software is not the "wrong" thing, but how one uses it could be wrong. It is easy to see how a statement that says "45 million people can't be wrong" can lead you to believe that IM, unquestionably, must be fine for your child to use. It is easy to see why your child will say, "Everyone has it!" or "You're ruining my social life!" if you do not allow your child to use something that 45 million other people use.

The message of Chapter 2 is important enough to be repeated: The relative newness of this fast-growing invention always needs to be considered. Compare the 45 million people scenario to a scenario with which you are more familiar and that has a lot more history and experience behind it. Here is some information about an activity that will remain anonymous for just a moment.

> About 10.1 million people age 12-20 years did this in the year 2001. The median age at which children begin doing this is 15.7 years old.

"Mom, Dad," says your child, "Everyone's doing it. I'm 15 years old. There are 10 million people around my age doing it. If you don't let me, you're ruining my social life!" Is that reason enough to allow them to partake? You would probably need to know what that activity is, and you would need to have more information about that activity.

The activity is underage drinking.[5] Most people are already aware of the health risks, the possibility of addiction, and the dangers of automobile and other drinking-related accidents. As parents, it is easier

---

[5]*Statistics and Resources: Youth Statistics,* <http://www.madd.org/under21/>. Mothers Against Drunk Driving, no date cited.

to make a decision about underage drinking because of the decades of history, precedent, research, and statistics. The same history, precedent, research, and statistics do not exist for the safe and ethical use of the internet because the internet is a relatively recent innovation. There is no widely-known, reputably established group like Mothers Against Drunk Driving (MADD) for the dangers of the internet. Some groups have begun commendable efforts, but in relative terms, we have only just begun. Because of the unprecedented fast growth, there is still a significant lack of laws, policies, and agencies to help protect and educate families.

"Everyone has it" or "Everyone is doing it" is not reason enough to allow your child to partake in an activity, particularly in a new field where safety and long-term effects are still in question. You cannot make a decision based on an advertisement about "45 million people."

Here is one more analogy to drive the point home. If a brand new drug came out that was not approved by the Food and Drug Administration (FDA), how would you go about making a decision on the use of that drug for your family? You may choose to find out more about the drug, allow use with precaution and restrictions, or not use it at all. Use the same precaution and care in making decisions about the internet. Millions of people probably would not flock to the drug until they have had a chance to see what side effects it may have. The internet's side effects are not immediate. They happen gradually, over a period of time. But the side effects are still there. Why not use the internet cautiously or wait to see the side effects before allowing free and open usage?

To close this section, here is a quote from the MADD website. Although it is about underage drinking and this book is about ethical online behavior, the underlying message crosses both realms. The experience and research of MADD have given them the wisdom to formulate these words. Perhaps we can learn from their experience. After all, is that not one of the reasons we value and learn about history? History helps us to preserve that which is important (our children, our values, our ethics), to learn from our mistakes, and to grow and move forward. At the very least, store this quote in your parental toolbox.

Regarding underage drinking - but also possibly true for children online without guidance – MADD states that underage drinking

> *"is more than a rite of passage. It's an invitation to clouded judgment, limited control and consequences that can last a lifetime."*[6]

Hidden Driver Example 2: Studies show . . .

Another pitfall is the "studies show" pitfall. This is true for just about any research study. Research and studies are invaluable and important. They provide excellent knowledge, resources, and foundational information to help us advance and make good decisions. You know that research can be valid and reliable, but it can also be intentionally or unintentionally skewed.

You pick up an article that states, "A study finds . . . use of technology increased math scores . . ."

You read the headline and perhaps a few more lines to discover that students who used the technology had better scores by 10% over those who did not use the technology. Your first reaction may be that now there is proof that technology really is necessary and good for learning and education. Therefore, you might conclude, your child must keep learning and growing with technology in order to have the best benefits possible. Is that necessarily true?

As an adult in this busy world, you do not have enough time in a day to read every article in its entirety in every newspaper or magazine. But do not let headlines and summaries mislead you. Although time does not allow you to find that research paper and verify the validity or reliability of the study, at the very least, step back for a moment and allow questions and possibilities to float through your mind.

The first and foremost question you should ask or at least wonder is "Who sponsored this study?" A university may have conducted it, but who paid for it? Was it a technology-based company? If so, they may

---

[6] *Under 21*, <http://www.madd.org/under21/>. Mothers Against Drunk Driving, no date cited.

have a vested interest in the outcome of the study. Could that have skewed the content or delivery of the study?

Other questions that should be asked include: Was the study thorough enough to include all possibilities? How was the study conducted? Did the study actually prove that it was indeed the technology that improved the scores? Were all variables considered? Did they make sure that the group that did better on the test did not just happen to be more mathematically inclined? Was it just the extra time and help that the technology provided, or was it actually the software program itself that improved the scores? What if they used a tutor or a supplemental book instead of technology? Would the results still have been at 10% better or maybe even more than 10%? Did they test for that variable? The questions are endless. Did the study provide for all possible variables and actually prove that which it claims?

As a trusting adult in this busy world, you do not have the time to find out all the details. But the headline sure did stick in your mind. Make note of the headline, but do not assume it is a proven fact. Instead, treat the headline or the outcome of the study as only a possibly helpful tool for you. Unless you know the details, it may not be prudent to put that "study shows" in your parental toolbox because it could be false or misleading. Research does have its place, and there are many reputable research projects. At the same time, the words "studies show" are often used as an advertisement tool. Put that information into your parental toolbox to remind you to evaluate the real value a study may have for your decision-making process.

Once again, know the source. At the very least, ask yourself, "I wonder who sponsored this study? What is the real purpose of this study? Did it really prove what it claimed?"

Hidden Driver Example #3: Internet – Capital I?

Here is a subtle yet powerful hidden driver.

Is the word "internet" supposed to have a capital I?

Chapter 5 – Knowledge Group 1: Know the Source

Not only is there no steadfast ruling on this question, but many debate this issue. Even several websites offer a debate forum on the issue. Some dictionaries list the entry with a capital I, while others do not. (It is interesting to note that most dictionaries did not even have the word "internet" listed until the late 1990's.) Technology companies generally use the capital I and also incorporate it into their spelling check dictionaries to dictate the use of a capital I.

Who started the use of the capital I? Could it have been the technology industry? The use of a capital letter generally gives a subtle hint of importance or unique standing. When you see the word internet written with a capital I, does it convey a sense of importance?

This book intentionally does not capitalize the word "internet." The internet is an excellent tool just like an encyclopedia, a dictionary, a calculator, an expert, or a book, none of which are capitalized.

As an adult in this new information age, be aware of the small, subtle nuances and choose to accept them in their real context. Who says the internet must be capitalized? Since there is a current debate, that must mean something. What does that mean for you? Place those thoughts in your parental toolbox.

Summary of "Know the Source"

The pressure to have the greatest, latest, and fastest technology is a result of everything from subtle grammar to subliminal or obvious advertising methods. The "need to know – need to have" stress creates a great deal of peer pressure regarding online activity. You should now be able to use your foundational knowledge to question, "What is the source?"

Know the source.
Or at least question it.

The pressure is not coming from educational research, learning theory, developmental stages, or doctors of psychology. The source is probably advertising and peer pressure. Do not allow those things to make safe and ethical decisions for your family. You make the decisions. You are not trying to make a buck and sell your family on a product. Therefore, you are the one who can make the best decisions for your family.

CHAPTER 6

Knowledge Group 2: Know the Question

Before you can make the best decisions for your family, identify the actual question you are trying to answer. The number of questions that arise from this confusing and intimidating issue tends to scare us away from addressing them. This chapter will help you put the multitude of questions on the table and then pinpoint the real, most important question. You can then address the real question.

Chapter 5 listed common pressures faced by many parents. These pressures are also the questions that parents face. How long? How much? At what age? How do I deal with my child's resistance? Is my child right? Am I just fighting the inevitable? Am I stuck in the Dark Ages? Am I holding her back? Am I obstructing or hindering her growth by placing limits?

Along with these questions come many dilemmas, which in this book will be nicknamed "To Be or Not To Be." That phrase is one of the most widely known expressions used to denote a dilemma. But it also serves as a subtle reminder of the contrast of the richness and depth of history (William Shakespeare) versus the shallow, less-explored nature of newer innovations (the internet).

To Be or Not To Be Dilemmas

Privacy vs. Parental Involvement

How much privacy should your child have while online? You do not want to be a nosey, overbearing parent. You believe in independence and respect privacy. Yet you hear so much about the ethical and safety dangers of children being online.

The dilemma: How much parental involvement should you have vs. how much privacy should they have?

Trust vs. Suspicion

You love your child. You trust your child. You hope that you have raised your child to be an honest, trustworthy, ethical citizen. Many believe that you have to give children trust in order for them to learn trust, to become trustworthy, and to respect the value of trust. If you put limits on your child's online activity, she may respond, "Don't you trust me?" You do not want to be suspicious, yet you hear so much about the safety problems in the online world. This book itself is about how online behavior is slowly transforming our society's ethics and morals one child at time. Your child is one of society's children. Where does your child fall in the scheme of things?

The dilemma: Where is the line between trust and suspicion?

Accidental vs. Intentional

You do trust your child. However, it is perfectly understandable how a child could accidentally run across an inappropriate website. As a matter of fact, it is almost unavoidable. You certainly cannot blame or punish a child for an honest accident. On the other hand, it is unrealistic to believe that every single child who "hits" an inappropriate website came upon it by accident. Was it intentional or was it an accident? Regardless, does easy, fast exposure to inappropriate pictures and words slowly chip away at our children's morals and ethics?

Take the accidental "hit" one step further. A child comes across an "Over 18" site, and curiosity takes over. Can you really blame a child for being curious? Curiosity is a normal, healthy aspect of growth, development, and even adulthood. But a child's inquisitiveness is not the only factor to consider. With a click of the mouse, a child can easily claim she is 18 years old to gain access to the site without anyone knowing it is a lie. What habits and morals does a child develop from effortless, unaccountable lies?

The accidental vs. intentional dilemma also pertains to ICE (Refer to Chapter 1). For example, a child is sitting alone, in the comfort of her own living room, and types an innocent email to a girlfriend about the school day. She thinks to herself, "... *and you really hurt my feelings when you sat next to that other girl at lunch. That was really ugly of you to do that to me.*" Her words are clear in her mind, but her abbreviated typed message comes out as, "Why did you sit next to that other girl. You are ugly." Although her intention was to say that her feelings were hurt and that she felt the behavior was unkind (ugly), the result is that her girlfriend reads, "You are ugly." Then it all begins . . . by accident. The virtual wall may have accidentally caused the misunderstanding, but it is now serving as an intentional hiding mechanism that allows mean things to be said that would not normally be said face-to-face.

The dilemma: How do you know if it is an accidental vs. intentional incident? How does the role of curiosity play in this dilemma?

Filtering Software vs. Not

This dilemma is closely tied to the first one: Privacy vs. Parental Involvement. The parental involvement mentioned in the first dilemma refers more to parents' physical and verbal involvement in their children's online activity. Filtering software, in this case, refers to installing and using a computer program to control and monitor online activity. There are many types of filtering software that help prevent accidental or intentional exposure to inappropriate websites by controlling the types of websites that are accessible. The software usually has different levels and options for parents to choose what they define as "inappropriate." There are also many options for parental control and monitoring of email activity.[7] This issue also goes hand-in-hand with the trust issue. Some families believe that if children are trusted, then there is no need for a software program that prevents and limits.

---

[7] Filtering and monitoring software is discussed more thoroughly in the next book. To find more about it now, an excellent resource is *Tools for Families*, <http://kids.getnetwise.org/tools/index.php>. GetNetWise, 1999-2003. Be sure to read the entire page, as the bottom half has an excellent tool for parents. Last accessed: September 2004.

At the same time, there is a disturbing concern about how children often know how to bypass filtering software. Children have learned to work around the controls, hack through the passwords, or disable the software so that they can access inappropriate sites or send and receive unmonitored emails. Likewise, parents are told that they can check the history files to see a list of visited websites, yet children easily learn how to delete those history files to hide the truth from their parents. Is there a double-edged sword here? On the one hand, you have a brilliant, technologically savvy child. On the other hand, she is using this brilliance for an ethically questionable behavior. Is the same software that is supposed to be protecting our children and providing an ethical platform giving them an opportunity to learn unethical behavior?

The dilemma: Do you use filtering software or not?

A Side Note

A company based in Florida is now providing intensive training for students to become expert hackers against hackers. Completion of the program earns them the title of "Certified Ethical Hacker."[8] Think about that title. Is it an oxymoron? What is it saying about the evolution of our society's ethics due to this free-for-all, worldwide, online access?

ICE vs. No ICE

As described in Chapter 1, ICE is:

I	Instant Messaging
C	Chat Room
E	Email

---

[8] *Ethical Hacking is No Oxymoron,*
<http://www.wired.com/news/infostructure/0,1377,64008,00.html>. Wired News, June 27, 2004.

Chapter 6 – Knowledge Group 2: Know the Question

ICE is a cold method of communication. A person's message and intended meaning are easily misinterpreted due to the absence of emotions, facial expressions, voice intonation, and other visual body language.

Faced with the ICE vs. No ICE dilemma, parents often hear, "But everyone is using it!" Naturally, parents wonder if the use of ICE is a necessity in the new millennium. They do not want to be "old-fashion fuddy duddies" who are stuck in the past. Nor do they want to impede their children's social growth and development.

But there is more to consider than just your child's social life with her buddies. For example, consider, once again, the innocence of curiosity. Curiosity can play an enormous role in chat rooms. A child wonders, *"What would it be like to act like I am a thirty-year-old woman?"* *"I wonder who this* Loves Kids *person is."* People in chat rooms almost always have pseudonyms. Surveys[9] have shown that most people not only change their names, but also change their real identities when in chat rooms.[10] Where will your child's curiosity lead her? Once the initial accidental encounter or curious adventure occurs, will there be future intentional use of pseudonyms? What is slowly happening to the morals and ethics of children who, in the quiet privacy of their own homes, are pretending to be someone else?

A child may be playing an innocent pretend game in her own mind as she sits sit alone in front of a computer. She is alone. It is pretend to her. She sees no one else. She may get feedback or typed words from the other person online on the computer screen. To her, the feedback may seem no different from a computer game that responds, "You scored, Lisa! Way to go!" The response is just typed letters on the screen.

---

[9] Here is your first opportunity to question "Surveys show . . ." In this case, the source is multiple not-for-profit and government agencies (see Additional Information section of this book) who are trying to help protect our children. No one is trying to sell a product.

[10] This is a serious issue. Adult predators pose as children to deceptively befriend other children. This safety issue is addressed in the next book about online safety. For information now on this topic, refer to the Additional Information section of this book.

No face, no person, no emotion, no voice intonation, and no real feelings can be seen or heard. But the feedback did not come from a computer program. A real person typed those letters on the screen. The person who responded is not pretend.

> When we adults were children, we may have had pretend, invisible friends. They were really pretend and invisible. But when a child plays "pretend" in a chat room with an online, invisible person, that person is not really invisible. That person is real.

Your child's seemingly innocent typing on a keyboard is affecting someone else's life and your child's own life. The computer game that spit out, "You scored, Lisa! Way to go!" has no feelings and is just a line of bits and bytes in a computer program. The chat room buddy who types, "I'm thirteen, too! I know how you feel," is not just a line of bits and bytes in a program.

Are our children really differentiating between the two? Are our children doing exactly what they would do if they were face-to-face with this chat room person? What type of ethical change is going on inside their minds as they are pretending to play pretend in a real world? Can we, as adults, even fathom this new concept of playing pretend with a real person in a real world?

The dilemma: Do you allow your child to have ICE or not?

Stand Back and Look at the Big Picture

Many questions and dilemmas have been asked and yet no answers have been given. You may have even come up with additional questions and dilemmas. Up to now, the questions and dilemmas have been about technology. How much? How often? What kind? Use it or not? Yes or no? Remember that technology has been "sold" to us by the technology industry. Therefore the source of all these questions came from the technology industry's excellent selling skills. But is the question really about technology? Stand back for a moment and look at the big picture. Forget about technology and examine the issue from a child-development perspective.

A Different Perspective

For example, take on the child-development viewpoint of Dr. Jane Healy. So as not to neglect the "Know the Source" motto, who is Dr. Jane Healy? In a nutshell, she was a professional educator and administrator, who signed on immediately with the technological craze in education. She took great pride in her contributions to a school system's technological advancements. But later, Dr. Healy realized that all the hoopla over technology was not the prize cow that it was built up to be. Dr. Healy is also an educational psychologist with a specialization in brain research and developmental growth and learning. Her expertise provides important data about human development based on research, history, precedent, and experience.

Dr. Healy provides a gold mine of treasures in her books and seminars. From those resources, there are three main points that are specifically relevant to the content of this book.

1.   Critical stages in human development

In her book, <u>Failure to Connect: How Computers Affect Our Children's Minds—and What We Can Do About It</u>, Dr. Healy discusses critical stages for certain areas of brain and human development during a child's growing years, such as gross and fine motor skills, depth perception, learning motivation, and personality, to name only a few. Time spent on a computer takes away time that could be spent on developing these skills and traits. *"If we waste or subvert these developmental windows, the losses may be irrecoverable."*[11]

Consider, then, some of the real, hands-on activities that are being replaced by computer time:

---

[11] <u>Failure to Connect: How Computers Affect Our Children's Minds—and What We Can Do About It</u>. Jane M. Healy, Touchstone, 1998.

- learning to run, skip, then run faster;
- learning to ride bikes;
- learning balance and coordination, "Look mom, no hands!" (and yes, learning to fall!);
- learning competition and cooperation with buddies;
- learning face-to-face, real-life, social interactions and skills.

Taking this a step further, time on a computer takes away from physical activity, which exacerbates the growing problem of overweight and obese children.[12] Time on a computer takes away family time. Could the lack of family time directly affect family values, ethics, and ties?

2. No critical technology learning age

In her book, Dr. Healy lists the critical ages and stages along with the associated skills and traits. The list does not mention a critical age for learning technology. Indeed, there is no proof of a specific age by which children need to learn technology. Today's adults are the best evidence to support that statement.

Today, in 2004, there are many adults, age thirty-five and older, who never touched a computer all through childhood and even perhaps all through college years (except for maybe those punch card programming classes!) The first time they touched a computer was at age twenty-two or even age thirty or forty. Yet they are highly computer literate. Many of them are the ones who created the most popular software packages today. Many of them are the experts who are teaching technology to our students today. Many of them never had email, IM, or chat rooms until they were in their thirties or forties, yet they are totally proficient users today.

---

[12] *"Today there are nearly twice as many overweight children and almost three times as many overweight adolescents as there were in 1980."* Nutrition and Physical Activity, <http://www.phsc.org/oo_faq.pdf>. National Center for Chronic Disease Prevention and Health Promotion, Public Health Student Caucus, December 9, 2003.

This is not to say that there has been a definite correlation between computer time and overweight/obese children. However, the study does note that barriers to an active lifestyle and not enough physical activity are reasons for overweight/obesity problems.

Chapter 6 – Knowledge Group 2: Know the Question

3. *Guinea pigs*

Dr. Healy uses the analogy of calling our children "Guinea Pigs." They are the guinea pigs of this new online age, often referred to as the Information Age. They are flying the Wright Brothers' planes without an FCC or traffic control center. They are navigating worldwide waters (surfing the net) without any quality or safety control agencies like the FDA, DOT, or Coast Guard. Without adequate history or precedent, we do not know what long-term effects[13] the computer will have on vision, posture, radiation, or even family time. We have already started seeing an ethical effect, hence this book.

Therefore, today's children are the guinea pigs. How much of a guinea pig are you willing to allow your child to be?

What is The Question?

The question is not about technology. It is not about how much, how many, when, what kind, or at what age. Although these are valid questions you may have, they are not the questions that need to be answered first. There will be help in addressing those questions in Chapters 8 & 10.

The real question is not about technology.
The question is about your family.

What is best for your family? What do you want for your family? What means the most to you for your family? Knowing that there are critical stages and ages of brain and growth development, what does that mean for your family? Knowing that there is no critical technology learning age, what does that mean for your family? Knowing that time on the computer takes away time from other valuable activities, what does that

---

[13] Long-term data is difficult to gather due to the relative newness of the internet as we know it today. However, researchers have begun to formulate consistent consensus and compelling cause-and-effect theories.

mean for your family? Knowing that your child is a guinea pig, what does that mean for your family?

You have been viewing this situation through the tinted, tainted glasses of technology. The purpose of this chapter was to remove those glasses to give you a different perspective from which to evaluate and make decisions.

> The decision is about your family.
> The decision is not about technology.

You are almost ready to start the decision-making process, but there is one more Knowledge Group to explore.

CHAPTER 7
Knowledge Group 3: Know the Environment

When you send your child to school, you know all about the school environment not only because you probably have checked it out, but also because you have been in school yourself. When you send your child to the movies, you know what the movie theater is like. When you allow your child online, do you know the environment?

What is the internet? What is the worldwide web? First it may be interesting to note that the word "internet" did not appear in most dictionaries until about 1997-98. Place that information into perspective and put it into your parental toolbox. In short, the internet is a

Worldwide Communications Computer Network

Think about those words for a moment. Chapter 6 tells us that the question and decision is about family, not technology. Change the above definition out of a technology perspective and into a family perspective. Perhaps the definition of the internet can now be viewed as

Anyone, Anytime, Anywhere

Now consider those words. When your child is on the internet, she is able to access anyone, anytime, anywhere in the world. Likewise, when your child is on the internet (and even when she is not!), anyone, anytime, anywhere in the world has access to her.

> The worldwide web has given your child access to the world.
> But it has also given the world access to your child.

It has given 729 million people access to your child. Take this online situation and make a direct comparison to something more concrete, something with which you have knowledge and experience. Since the question is about your family and not technology, put this technological concept into a family perspective. Here are two analogies to help you get started.

Two Analogies to Consider

1. *Adult stores and movies*

Do you allow your school-aged child to go to the movie theater by herself whenever she wants to go? Do you allow her to go to X-rated movies by herself, whenever she wants? Do you allow your child to walk into adult bookstores or adult video stores by herself, whenever she wants? Of course not. Why not? There are a number of reasons, including safety issues as well as the moral, ethical, and character repercussions of exposing a young child to inappropriate material.

Would you take your child to a mall that had adult book/video stores or X-rated movies and allow her to wander on her own? There is a chance she could accidentally wander into the store or movie theater. Luckily, however, there will be store attendants and movie theater employees that will recognize that she is underage and stop her.

Allowing your child to surf online without guidelines, supervision, or some type of adult involvement is no different than allowing your child to wander around adult bookstores and X-rated movies. Actually there is one difference. There are no attendants or employees to stop her from accidentally accessing inappropriate material on the internet. You are giving your child free, open access to the world. Even if your child is 100% trustworthy, the "anyones" of the world have made it incredibly convenient and easy to accidentally bump into inappropriate sites.

Now imagine your child walking into these adult stores every day. Curiosity kicks in, and she explores all the different materials and movies. What impact will that have on her moral and ethical nature? What impact will that have on her growth and development? What impact will that have on her?

Further, we have not even begun to consider what strangers she will encounter in these stores and movie theaters. That topic is part of the larger safety issue but needs to be recognized as you consider this analogy.

2. *Toys*

In talking about the internet and children, safety and ethics go hand in hand (right along with crime). This second analogy also has both safety and ethical relevance.

Hopefully, most parents have seen some of the basic rules about children and the internet. They are often called the "Online Safety Rules" or "The Rules of the Road."[14] There are hundreds of websites and books that provide a list of these helpful strategies. Here is a summary list of just a few of the most commonly known rules.

~ Never give out personal information or pictures without parental permission.

~ Don't talk to strangers online.

~ Never agree to meet an online friend in person without parental permission.

~ Tell parents about anyone or anything that makes you feel uncomfortable.

~ Don't respond to email or messages that are mean or inappropriate, or that contain bad language.

For parents, the number one rule is always to place a computer with internet access in a family room, not in a child's room.

Once again, remember the question and decision is about your family, not technology. Put the above information into a familiar family

---

[14] The Additional Information section of this book provides an example of these rules along with further resources to learn more about them.

scenario. You go to the toy store to buy a bike, scooter, or any other toy for your child. You read the instructions or label on the outside of the package. Often, it will include some warnings such as "Remove and dispose of plastic," or "Not recommended for children under the age of 5."

What if you picked up a toy and the instructions included these words:

> Never Never Don't Don't
> Strangers
> Uncomfortable
> Mean
> Inappropriate
> Bad language

The last line says, "Not recommended for use in a child's room."

Would you buy that toy?

Purpose of the Two Analogies

Cyberspace is not something you can reach out and touch. It is a concept. The two analogies were used to help you put that concept into real terms. The online world is real. The people on the other end of your child's computer are real. The dangers are real. The decline in the ethical fiber of our society and children is real.

The purpose of the analogies is:

~ NOT for you to run, run, run away as fast as you can!

~ NOT to have you respond, "The internet is way too dangerous. My child will never be allowed on it again."

The purpose of the analogies:

~ IS to provide a family perspective on the situation.

~ IS to pull you out of the sea of technological waves that have been drowning your ability to make the best decisions for your family.

~ IS to have you respond, "The internet is dangerous. How can I best allow my child to be in an 'anyone, anytime, anywhere' environment, yet preserve her integrity and safety?"

The purpose of the analogies is the title of this chapter -- to help you understand and Know the Environment in order to make the best decisions for your family.

More About The Environment – Laws

Now take a look at this online world in terms of the government and laws. It has already been acknowledged that there are no standard governing national agencies (like the FDA or FCC), to help protect the safety and ethics of adults, much less children, online. The issue has not been ignored. Many individuals, groups, and agencies like the Department of Justice and the FBI have addressed the issue and provide excellent family information (see Additional Information section). There have been some successful and some unsuccessful attempts to create laws to help protect our children. But these attempts still fall short. Here are just two examples.

1. COPPA – Child Online Privacy Protection Act

The purpose of COPPA is to protect the privacy of children under the age of 13. In 1996, there was a report about the intentional and *"abusive online marketing and data collection practices directed at children."*[15] As a result, in 1998, COPPA was signed into law. The law did not take effect until April 2000.

---

[15]*A Parent's Guide to Online Privacy*, <http://www.misspixel.com/kids/history.html>. Center for Media Education Privacy Policy, no date cited.

Thoughts to ponder:

~ What about children 13 and older? What about their privacy?

~ What does this say about the ethics of those businesses who were trying "to make a buck"? A law had to be enacted to maintain some ethical standards. Did they lose sight because it was so easy to utilize "abusive online marketing" techniques? Did they lose sight because they never had "sight" of the young children on the other end of the computer?

~ What does this do to the ethics of children age 13 and older? Does this provide temptation toward an unethical behavior? A 13-year-old generally cannot use a credit card by herself in a store to purchase a $3,000 stereo. However, online it is very easy for a 13-year-old to make purchases with credit cards that have been stolen from her parents or others.

~ The law prevents businesses from purposely going after children under the age of 13. But the law does not prevent children under the age of 13 from lying or pretending that they are of age. What temptations does that create?

2. **COPA – Child Online Protection Act**

In October 1998 Congress created the Child Online Protection Act (COPA) for the purpose of protecting the physical and psychological well-being of minors from harmful online material. The Act established a Commission on Online Child Protection to study *"methods to help reduce access by minors to material that is harmful to minors on the Internet."*[16] The Commission's final report stated that even innovative methods, such as parental controls and self-regulation, were not addressing the problem. Children are still being exposed to harmful materials. COPA was never enforced because it was challenged as unconstitutional. The challenge was upheld by the Supreme Court. The attempt to protect our children failed.

---

[16] *Welcome to COPACommission.org,* <http://www.copacommission.com>. COPA Commission, 2000.

It is disheartening that the attempt failed. But those who challenged COPA had a legitimate, constitutional basis for their challenge. (Since the defeat of COPA, other smaller-scale attempts to protect our children have been made.[17]) The debate over COPA magnifies the fact that the fast-paced growth of the internet has even attorneys, prosecutors, judges, and the law struggling to keep up. Cyberspace whirled into existence almost instantly, but figuring out how our society can and should exist within it is going to take some time. Finding solutions is a process and a long one at that. In the meantime, as our country struggles to find viable methods to protect our children while online, you as the parent have the first and foremost responsibility.

These are just two examples of attempts to help protect our children with laws. There are other similar ones.[18] The successful ones still carry with them many questions and a need for fine-tuning and improvement. The unsuccessful ones mean, once again, that today's young children are the guinea pigs.

Summary

Cyberspace is a relatively new place. It is an "anyone, anytime, anywhere" environment. As the country and laws push hard to keep up, remember that your child is swimming in uncharted waters. You are the only lifeguard or life jacket for your child. Just because there are millions treading in these waters does not mean that it is safe. As a matter fact, the existence of millions makes the waters even more dangerous.

Now that you know the environment and you have a general feeling of the depth, turbulence, and vastness of the water, you can begin to start making decisions for your family.

---

[17] Other measures have been put in place, such as the "Over 18" question required on pornographic sites and the Dot Kids Act. However, those measures are only a small step forward that merely scratches the surface of the problem. No solutions, to date, adequately protect minors from easy accessibility to harmful material.

[18] For other laws regarding children: <http://access.k12.wv.us/manual/urlfeder.htm>. Last accessed: July 2004. Resources on laws concerning businesses, homes, and online crimes can be found in the Additional Information section of this book.

CHAPTER 8
Making Decisions for Your Family

You are now ready to start the decision-making process. The previous chapters have presented information for you to use to make decisions for your family that are not based on fear, peer pressure, industry pressure, or other misleading data. What exactly are you deciding?

> Since I am responsible for my child in the online world, what guidelines do I need to provide for her to help preserve the ethical integrity of my family and society?

Notice first that the question stated above is about your family and not technology. Every answer you give should be about your family. Perhaps the first words of each answer should be, "For the best benefit of my family . . ."

The decision is about your family, but the topic is technology. Therefore, questions about technology cannot be ignored or excluded from the process. To answer the big question stated above, you must address the underlying questions about technology. Here are some of the questions that have already been identified. Add your questions to the list:

~ How much time should I allow my child to spend online?
~ At what age should my child be online?
~ What rules should I have?
~ What about all the To Be or Not To Be dilemmas in Chapter 6?

The Three-Step Process

There are many ways to make the best decision for your family. At this point, if you feel prepared to start making decisions, do it. If you would like a little more guidance, this chapter will provide instructions for a three-step process. Chapter 10 provides a template for you to use. Following is an overview of each step.

Step 1 - Pulling It All Together

Take all the information in Chapters 1-7 and pull it all together. Chapters 1-7 took you a step back and placed the situation into a non-technical perspective. Diagram 8-1 provides a visual of this step in the process.

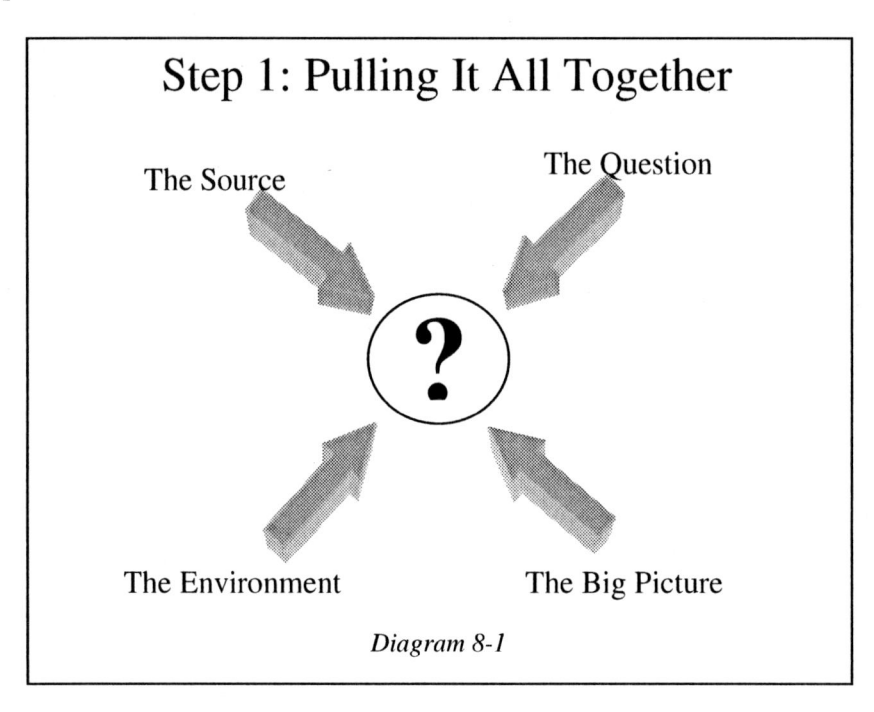

Step 1: Pulling It All Together

The Source → ? ← The Question
The Environment ↗ ? ↖ The Big Picture

Diagram 8-1

The Source:	Know that it is the technology industry that is the driving force, not years of proven research.
The Question:	Know that the question is about your family, not technology.
The Environment:	Know that the internet is an anyone/anytime/anywhere environment with laws in the process of being made.
The Big Picture:	Know that the whirlwind arrival of the internet should not scare you into thinking you have to be an internet expert in order to guide your child in uncharted waters.

Chapter 8 - Making Decisions for Your Family

In Diagram 8-1, notice that when you pull all the information together, all the identified knowledge should focus in on one central piece. This has been the missing piece all along, since the birth of the internet. You will notice that the same essential piece is missing in the next two steps.

Step 2 - Balancing the Scale

A family can decide to ban the use of the internet completely in their home. However, that may not be realistic, nor is it the purpose of this book. The internet provides excellent opportunities which should not be discounted or ignored. Instead, in dealing with the questions of how long, how much, what age, and the To Be or Not To Be dilemmas, families should make a balanced decision based on the solid foundation (Diagram 8-2). What is the solid foundation? At this point, the foundation is the missing piece.

Step 2: Balancing the Scale

Balance your decision on a solid foundation.

Diagram 8-2

Step 3 - Sailing the Net

A water analogy has been used throughout this book because the internet is a world of both safe and hazardous waters. Like water, it has its benefits and its dangers. Like water, it is a vast ocean of opportunity. Like water, it is becoming a key component of our lives. We really cannot ignore it, but we can learn to navigate it safely. Unlike water, the internet has no Coast Guard and no internationally recognized rules and regulations for safe and proper use.

The water analogy has already been set in place with the relatively popular phrase, "Surf the Net." (A search on the internet for that phrase resulted in over four million hits.) Picture your child in Hawaii surfing enormous, powerful waves. Picture her surfing without lessons, without a lifeguard, and without any guidance. Now picture your child in the water but not surfing powerful waves. Instead, she is sailing with life rafts, life jackets, lessons on how to sail, and guidelines. This book recommends that your family "Sail the Net" (Diagram 8-3) rather than "Surf the Net."[19] Sailing the net allows your family to be in the exact same waters (the worldwide web) as are the surfers. It allows them to gain the same benefits and have the same opportunities, but in a more family-oriented environment.

When you have your child "Sail the Net," what do you use as your sails?

The Missing Piece

What is the missing piece and why was it intentionally omitted? In Chapter 2, it was acknowledged that today's parents have no "passed down" wisdom about the internet. Although our grandparents and

---

[19] An interesting note: "Surf the Net" resulted in over four million hits. The top ten hits were about internet usage. "Sail the Net" resulted in 85% fewer hits. Eight out of the top ten were about boats, marine supplies, and sailors, not about the internet. Why is "Sail the Net" not as popular? Could it be something as simple as a "take off" from TV channel surfing? TV channel surfing even has its dangers with possible exposure to inappropriate language or images. But at least TV surfing does not involve real, live interaction with a person on the other side. Is "Sailing" not popular because it is not "cool," "extreme," or "in"? Says who?

parents did not know about the internet, they did pass down some very valuable wisdom. They gave us "the missing piece."

Step 3: Sailing the Net

Diagram 8-3

The missing piece is the MVP. MVP, not coincidentally, has two meanings:

        MVP = Most Valuable Person(s)

        MVP = Morals, Values, Principles

In all of the hoopla and noise about the internet, little attention has been given to your MVPs. Your most valuable person (child) and your family's morals, values, and principles should be at the center (Diagram 8-4) of your decisions. They should be the foundation upon which to make balanced decisions (Diagram 8-5). They should be the driving force behind your child's adventures (Diagram 8-6).

Chapter 8 - Making Decisions for Your Family

Step 1: Pulling It All Together

The Source

The Question

Your MVPs

The Environment

The Big Picture

Diagram 8-4

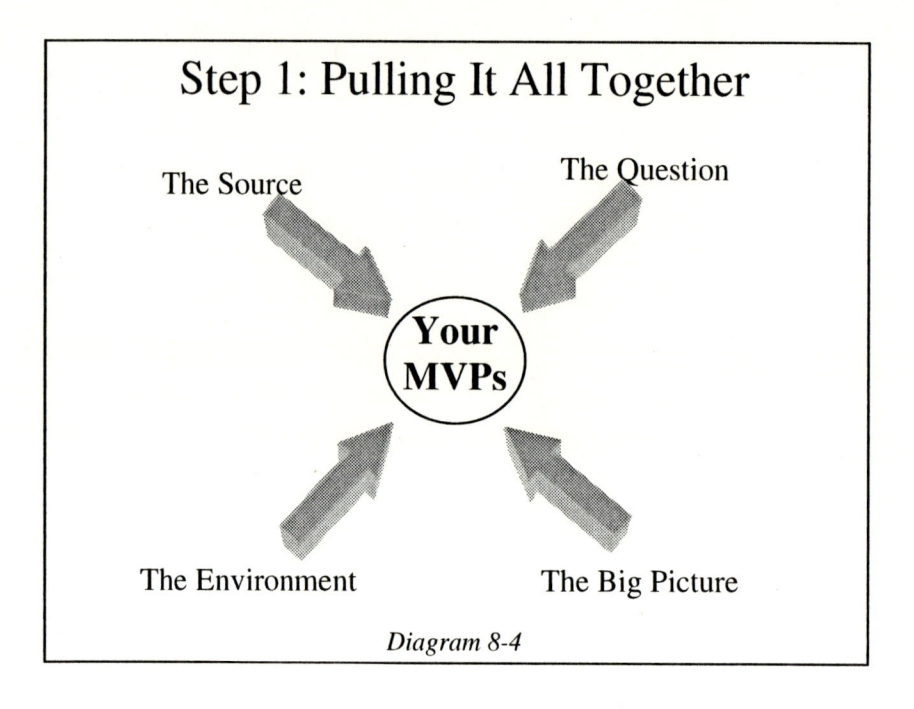

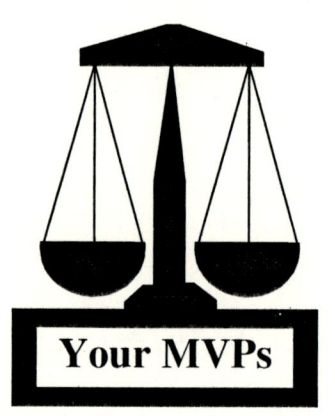

Step 2: Balancing the Scale

Your MVPs

Balance your decision on a solid foundation.

Diagram 8-5

Chapter 8 - Making Decisions for Your Family

Step 3: Sailing the Net

Your MVPs

Diagram 8-6

The missing piece was intentionally missing at the start of this chapter because it is missing from the technical jargon and pressure. In all the push for faster, greater, and more, no one mentions your MVPs. Instructional books on how to use technology do not usually come with a chapter on your MVPs. When you download or install software, you are given a copyright notice that safeguards and protects the vendor's profit, but there is no notice included that safeguards or protects your MVPs.

Therefore it is up to you, the parent, to place your MVPs in the center, to make your MVPs the foundation of all decisions, and to choose to make your MVPs the driving force.

How Do You Do That?

Many people may be on the "look out" for a simple, canned answer, but there is no one-answer method. There is no "best" way to raise a child. Every family has their own unique method based on the school of thought and psychology to which they subscribe. Likewise, there is no one-answer method for decisions on technology and the internet. It all depends on your beliefs, on your morals, values, and principles for

Chapter 8 - Making Decisions for Your Family

your family. On one end of the spectrum is not to allow your child to use the internet at all. On the other extreme is to give her free rein without any limitations or guidelines. You may choose one of those ends or you may fall somewhere in between the two extremes.

Before you can apply your MVPs to the three-step process (note that it is a process, not a final answer), you need to identify your MVPs. The first part is easy. The most valuable person in this scenario is your child. The second part is where the differences begin to separate your decisions from other families' decisions. Your morals, values, and principles probably differ from other families' to some degree. This is why the "But everyone has it" and "Everyone does it" arguments do not hold water (pun intended). "Everyone" does not have the exact same MVPs as you do.

Most families put safety first, but each family has a varying degree of tolerance regarding risk factors. Some are big risk takers, while others are not. Most families want their children to be good, ethical citizens, but each family has its own definition of what it takes to be ethical. You identify your own personal definition of ethics and your level of safety based on your morals, values, and principles.

> The word "your" is used repetitively because you must make a decision for your family based on your MVPs, not those of others.

You already know your MVPs. They were passed down to you and then molded and shaped to fit your family today. Chapter 10 suggests you write them down. Replace the missing piece in the three steps with your MVPs.

Step 1 - Place your MVPs in the center of your decisions.

The four arrows in Diagram 8-4 remind you that you do not need to be a technological expert. You do not need to know how to use the internet in order to make decisions about it. The knowledge you need is non-technical, and now you have all the tools. As you consider the information you know, answer any questions with your MVPs in the center. Here are some examples of how to place your MVPs at the center of your decisions.

Knowledge	MVPs in the Center
The technology industry is the driving force behind the pressure to have the latest, greatest, and fastest technology.	Use your MVPs to decide what is right, safe, and essential for your family.
Just because everyone is doing "it," does not mean "it" is right, safe, or essential.	

Knowledge	MVPs in the Center
There is no critical technology-learning age.	Based on your MVPs, how much and what are you willing to replace?
There are critical human developmental learning stages.	
Time spent online replaces time spent on other activities.	

Knowledge	MVPs in the Center
The internet came on suddenly and grew at an unprecedented exponential rate.	How much of a guinea pig are you willing to allow your MVP (child) to be?
Today's children are the pioneers.	
Your child is a guinea pig.	

Knowledge	MVPs in the Center
The internet does provide excellent opportunities.	What level of risk are you willing to take in exchange for these opportunities?[20] Use your MVPs to balance your decision without compromising your MVPs.
Your child can sail the net and benefit from these opportunities.	

---

[20] The Chinese heritage has a long and rich history. We, too, can learn from its ancestors and wisdom. It is interesting to note that the Chinese symbol for "crisis" is a combination of the characters for opportunity and danger. How do you respond to a crisis? Here you have advance notice to choose to take the opportunity and minimize and perhaps almost omit the danger, thereby avoiding the crisis.

Chapter 8 - Making Decisions for Your Family

Knowledge	MVPs in the Center
Your child is not protected by a regulating body like the FDA, FCC, or Coast Guard.	Think about your child in a real body of water. What would your MVPs dictate?
You are her only lifeguard, lifeboat, and life jacket.	
The responsibility is 100% yours, the parent, but there are helpful resources.	

Knowledge	MVPs in the Center
When your child is online, she has access to the world.	Think about your child standing in the middle of 729 million people. What would your MVPs dictate?
The world also has access to her – anyone, anytime, anywhere, even in the safety of your own home.	

The decisions you are making are about your family (MVPs), not about technology. Your child's psychological and physical well-being is dependent upon you, your personal wisdom, and your inherited wisdom. The psychological and physical well-being of your child should not be decided by peer pressure, limited research, or advertising. There is a good reason why fifteen-year-olds are not allowed to drink, drive, vote, or go to war. The reason has to do with the experience, wisdom, developmental stages, and safety of those who have had a limited amount of exposure to life at that age.

Step 2 - Make a balanced decision based on your MVPs.

Make your MVPs the foundation on which to make a balanced decision on any technology-based question. Change the technology question into a family MVP question. For example, common questions about technology are:

~ How long?
~ How much?
~ At what age?

Chapter 8 - Making Decisions for Your Family

Since we now know that there is no magical age or magical number of hours to allow your child to be online or on the computer, consider these family MVP factors:

~   How important is physical activity to your family?

~   How much time do you allow them *in front of* the television?

~   Will you have a total number of *in front of* hours which include both the TV and the computer?

~   How concerned are you about the long-term radiation, posture, and visual effects of *in front of* time?

~   Where is the balance between online time and outside time?

~   Is there some activity more valuable to you (family time, chores, physical activity) that should not be replaced with *in front of* time?

~   Is there some activity less valuable to you that can be replaced with *in front of* time?

~   There is no critical technology learning age. What is most important for them to develop at what ages? What can be sacrificed and at what level?

~   Your child will probably need to be on the computer for school work. Does that suffice to fill the need for computer time? Does that balance the scale?

Now you can do the same with the To Be or Not To Be dilemmas from Chapter 6. One of the issues listed is Trust vs. Suspicion. Many parents are faced with that decision because of the commonly heard cry, "Don't you trust me?" The answer is:

Trust is not the issue.

Your child can be 100% trustworthy and honest. Your child can be 0% trustworthy. It does not matter. Trust is not the issue. Some parents respond, "Honey, I trust you. It's the rest of the world that I don't trust." That is indeed one way to respond, but again, trust is not the issue.

The "rest of the world" is not even asking for your trust. The rest of the world does need or want your trust. The rest of the world does not consider trust as the issue. The criminals, pedophiles, pornographic publishers, and advertisers are not trying to be trustworthy. They do exactly what they do on purpose. They purposely set themselves up to make it very easy to land on their websites "accidentally." They purposely set themselves up to lure innocent children and adults. They purposely take the time to understand the psychology and traits of a thirteen-year-old girl, and they purposely use that information, knowing that they can "get to" a thirteen-year-old girl who is 100% trusted by her parents. After all, children are young, naïve, trusting of the world, innocent, and the easiest prey because they have not had enough years on this earth to truly understand the possibilities. Intruders know this and purposely plan accordingly. They are not asking for your trust. Trust is not the issue.

Yet, some parents may still wonder, "Why does this matter, if I trust my child?" Children who are 100% trustworthy will indeed do their 100% best to avoid inappropriate sites. They will approach a parent if they receive bad emails, feel uncomfortable with any communication, or are approached by a stranger online. Trust, still, is not the issue. The issue is not about the trustworthiness of your child.

What is the issue? The issue is that the internet is a money-making enterprise. It is not just a nice, free resource for people to use. More importantly, it is a business where two-thirds of the revenue comes from sex-related content. A report from Reuters Business Insight in February 2003

> "calculated that sex-related business represented two-thirds of all revenue generated by online content in 2001 and that it had ballooned to a $2.5 billion industry since then."[21]

---

[21] *Supreme Court keeps Net porn law on ice*, <http://news.com.com/2100-1028_3-5251475.html>. Declan McCullagh, CNET News.com, June 29, 2004.

Chapter 8 - Making Decisions for Your Family

The issue is that our children are playing in a worldwide playground that is purposely filled with sex-related content. With two-thirds of revenue generated by sex-related material, inappropriate sites are not the occasional exception but are, perhaps, the rule. Also, who are these criminals, predators, pedophiles, and unethical advertisers? Some are children! Some are adults. These adults were once children, just as your child is now. When they were children, they probably did not expect or plan to become a criminal or a questionable advertiser.

They are learning that cold ICE is the way to communicate and that hiding behind a wall is acceptable behavior because they do not have to face the consequences of words or actions that occur online. Online crime is a growing problem (see "Cultivating Criminals?" in the Additional Information section). Is it growing because more and more people are learning poor ethical behavior online? Is your child learning that cold ICE is the way to communicate because she can hide behind a wall and not have to face the consequences of words or actions that occur online? In what direction do you want to steer your child?

Remember that today, right now, we are cultivating future criminals. If you have not read "Cultivating Criminals?" in the Additional Information section, read it now.

The decisions you are making today are not just affecting your family; they are affecting the future of society.

Whatever you teach your child today is exactly what she will be passing down to her children. Today's children are the guinea pigs of the internet. Today's adults are the guinea pigs of the parental challenges posed by the internet. Someone, somewhere, somehow has to hold steadfast to the moral integrity of society. It can only be done one family at a time. You are a family. Therefore, it must start with you.

Chapter 8 - Making Decisions for Your Family

Step 3 - Sail the net with your MVPs.

Once you have made your decisions based on your MVPs, this third part flows naturally. You have set up your family's online life exactly the way you want it to be, not the way the world wants it to be. Write a set of basic family rules (see Additional Information section for an example). You can now safely sail the waters with your Most Valuable Person using your Morals, Values, and Principles as your driving force (Diagram 8-6).

Application: Making the Decisions

Some people may have been looking for standard guidelines or canned answers. Perhaps it would seemingly make it easier if someone would just tell you, "Children should not get online until age X." "Children in elementary school should only be on the computer Y hours per week." "ICE should not be allowed until age Z." Standard guidelines and canned answers would go against the grain of our society's basic principles of freedom and choice. Whoever would create standard guidelines would put their own personal biases and values upon those guidelines. Every family has their own set of values, and they must apply them to form the best decisions for their children. Furthermore, each school and school system has different perspectives on computer usage. This makes it impossible to create standard time limits or schedules that would satisfy all schools across the nation.

Here we are again, stating that it is the parent's responsibility. As a family in the land of the free, take advantage of this freedom to apply your MVPs in making the best decisions for your own family.

The decision-making process is relatively simple if you take it step-by-step. The process is not big or overwhelming and should not be put off until tomorrow. You can easily draft a rough copy or even a final copy right now. Chapter 10 provides one suggested outline for you to follow. Sometimes it is helpful, though, to hear about other families and have varying perspectives to help you get started. Therefore, Chapter 9 provides three personal stories from three real families.

CHAPTER 9
Three True Stories

This chapter provides three real-life stories about the Smiths, the Joneses, and Me. The two families are real, but the names are fictional. The conversations are not exact quotes, but they tell the story accurately. You might relate to one of the stories. You might not relate at all. You might agree or disagree with the families' decisions. The purpose of sharing these stories is to give you a springboard from which to start your own plan and to reinforce the concept that you are in charge of making decisions for your family.

The Smiths: "Mom! You're ruining my social life!"

Mrs. Smith heard a seminar on all the material you just read in Chapters 1-8. She decided it was time to make decisions for her two sons, Joe, age 11, and John, age 14. She was from "the old school," as some people affectionately name it. She believed very strongly in children playing and running. Having had brothers, she knew how much boys love to run around, how they skin knees, and how they break bones. Yes, it was a physically painful way to learn, but she believed it was part of the growing-up process. Yet her sons had perfect knees since they were spending hours surfing the net and using ICE instead of playing outside.

John surfaced from his room and exasperatedly said, "Girls!"

Mom: "What?"

John: "I'm so over them."

Mom: "What happened?"

John: "I just broke up with Rebecca."

Mom: "I thought you just broke up with that other girl."

John:	"Yeah, I did. Then Rebecca came along. She was cool. But now, not so much."
Mom:	"What did she say when you broke up with her?"
John:	"I don't know."
Mom:	"What do you mean, you don't know?"
John:	"After I said I didn't want to see her anymore, I just logged off."
Mom:	"What? You broke up with her online?"
John:	"Mom! Everyone does it. It's no big deal."

Mrs. Smith realized that her children were learning to hide behind the virtual wall of cyber space. John did not have to face Rebecca's reaction or feelings. Mrs. Smith knew it was easy to hurt someone online unintentionally, but it struck her hard that her son did it intentionally, knowing he did not have to face the consequences. She worried about the habits and mentality that could be forming in John's personality. Mrs. Smith made the following decisions:

~   No chat rooms.

~   No IM.

~   Email was allowed, but the children's personal email accounts had to go through the mom's account first. It was not that the parents wanted to read every email. In fact, they did not. It was the fact that all email that transpired should be "readable" by the parents.

~   The computer was moved into the family room. Filtering software was placed on the computer.

~   The children should only be online when there was an adult in the house.

Chapter 9 – Three True Stories

The reaction went something like this:

John: "Don't you trust us?"

Mom: "Yes, I do! I trust that you will not try to bypass the filtering software. I trust that you will tell me if you come across anything that doesn't feel or seem right. I trust that you will follow the rules. I trust that you know in your heart that I am doing this because of how much I love you and trust you."

John: "Mom! You're ruining my social life!"

Mom: "I understand you think I'm ruining your social life. I may be ruining your cyber social life, but I am saving your real life."

John: "Just because you didn't have the internet when you grew up doesn't mean that we have to live by the same standards. Mom, get with the new millennium."

Mom: "In your words, son, 'I am so with it.' More with it than you want."

John: "Great, now I have no social life."

Mom: "If you want a social life, pick up the phone and call your buddies. Invite people over to hang out or go outside. Play a sport or join a school activity and socialize before and after practices and meetings. Have a post-game party and socialize then. Do things that require a physical effort."

John: "I'm going to be such a nerd."

The resistance continued. Mrs. Smith knew that John might think he was a nerd now, but he would benefit more greatly in the long run, as an adult and for the rest of his life. She knew her sons would not stop arguing their case. She understood their perspective, but it was up to her to do what she thought was best for the family.

A year later, Mrs. Smith reported that her sons dramatically reduced their *in front of* time. The restrictions she placed made the computer a little less enticing. They did their homework on the computer as needed. They sailed now and again for fun, but overall, they spent more time doing other things. "It's amazing," she said, "John spends a lot of time reading now. I had no idea he was an avid reader. I don't think he knew that he was an avid reader, either!"

The children started to understand and realize what mom was doing. Each year, she allowed for a little more online activity. John, now a junior in high school, is allowed some IM time with guidelines. Her children are physically healthy. They are continuing to make excellent grades at school. They have developed new interests. They have learned to be accountable for their actions and not to hide behind a wall. They have many friends and are quite popular due to their active involvement and, ironically, due to their social skills. Most important, they still love their mom!

The Joneses: A Progressive Family

Mr. and Mrs. Jones are well-educated adults who are closely involved in their children's lives. Mr. Jones was a principal of a neighborhood school in a very affluent area. His family was progressive and embraced changes as opportunities to advance. The Jones family recognized and supported the use of technology and the internet for all the benefits it provides. The Joneses did have a family meeting about online safety, where they set up the basic "Rules of the Road."

Peter, age 11, Paul, age 9, and Mary, age 5, were all very good, respectful children. They agreed to the family rules about the internet. The family did not install filtering software but asked their children to inform the parents if they ran into inappropriate sites. The definition of an inappropriate site was clearly defined. Peter was allowed to use IM, but he had no interest. Paul was allowed to use IM, but only with his buddies. Mary was just learning to read and write, so IM was not an option for her.

Chapter 9 – Three True Stories

This arrangement seemed to be working fine until two incidents occurred. One day Mrs. Jones opened the browser to go on the internet and an inappropriate site came up as the main (home) page. Peter was the last one to be on the computer.

Mom: "Peter, how did this happen?"

Peter: "Mom, I honestly don't know."

Mom: "I thought I told you to tell me anytime you accidentally came across an inappropriate site."

Peter: "Mom, honestly, if a bad site comes up, I click off of it immediately. It happens so much I didn't want to bother you every time. But I promise that I follow the family rules."

Mrs. Jones did believe her son because of his high moral integrity. But how did this happen?

It happens because the programmers make it happen. It is easy to develop a site that makes itself your homepage. Mrs. Jones does not need to understand how it happens. She does not need to know the technical explanation. She does need to know that these types of things do happen, they happen easily, and as Peter said, they happen often.

Meantime, Paul walked around with his head drooped.

Mom: "What's up?"

Paul: "Nothing."

Mom: "Something's up or I wouldn't have had to ask."

Paul: "Oh, no biggie. My friends at school are kind of ignoring me."

Mom: "Why?"

Paul: "I don't know."

As it turns out, Paul's former buddy had gone on IM and pretended to be Paul. The buddy wrote some unkind things to Paul's friends. Since they all thought it was Paul who wrote these ugly messages, no one was talking to him. Eventually the confusion was cleared up for Paul, although the buddy always denied it, as there was no proof. Luckily most friendships were repaired, but some uneasiness remained.

The parents' perspective was that it was an unfortunate situation, feelings were hurt, and friendships were temporarily tarnished. Since hurt feelings happen in real life social scenarios as well, they viewed this as part of the learning and growing process. This was the second IM incident that occurred for Paul within his circle of friends. A similar first mishap occurred six or seven months ago. But the parents felt that neither occurrence was significantly detrimental; therefore, Paul was allowed to continue using online communication.

Comparing the Two

The two families have different perspectives. The Smiths and the Jones are both 100% correct in their decisions because it works for them and their families. In these stories, no crimes were committed. No one's safety was jeopardized. How does your family resemble or not resemble these families. Where do you agree or disagree? Reflect on the impact that these situations may have on your child's development of morals and ethics. What will it do to or for her future?

Me

This last story is about me and my personal perspective. In seminars and discussions, parents always ask me, "What do you suggest we do?"

I always answer, "You have to use your MVPs to make the best decision for your family. My MVPs may not be the same as yours. What works for me may not work for you."

The bottom line is that families are just asking for my personal opinion. They want to know how I live my life in this online world. I can reasonably guess that you may want to know the same thing. This third story, therefore, is about me. Before I begin, you should realize the extent of technology in my life (another example of Know the Source).

A Little Background

I love technology. I use it daily. I go online to get all types of forms from the government and other companies. I renew memberships online. I order almost everything online, including books, gifts, flowers, even clothes, makeup, and other such items. The convenience of the internet saves me a great deal of time and gives me many more options than if I visit just one store.

A Side Note

> Internet fraud is a huge international problem. It is impossible to accurately track the loss because not everyone reports it. In 2001, the total loss from all reported cases was $17 million. In 2002, it was $54 million. That is more than a 200% increase in one year.[22]

> I mentioned that quick note, because I do not want you to think that just because I do financial interactions online, it is completely safe. I know technology, and therefore, I know how to be careful. Since I am aware of the risks, I can avoid them more easily. I have set up safeguards, rules, and procedures to make it a safer platform for me to use.

I call myself a geek. When I go on vacation, I find a way to get online every day. Some family members claim that I'm an addict. On my recent five-day vacation to the beach, the hotel's public internet was "down." I drove to a nearby public coffee house that had internet

---

[22]*IFCC Internet Fraud Report*, <http://www.ifccfbi.gov/strategy/statistics.asp>. The Internet Fraud and Complaint Center, 2002.

access, and as I started walking into the store, I realized that my family was right. I was an addict! I didn't go in, and I stopped that behavior. I use email daily. I have IM. I have never been in a chat room and have no desire to do so. I have taught technology courses to children in Pre-Kindergarten through college and also to adults.

A Funny Anecdote

I started teaching technology in 1984. (For those of you who are of the old technology school, you'll laugh to know that I taught DOS 2.x.) Microsoft Windows only existed in its most infant form, but no one had heard of it yet. When I taught the MS-DOS courses, I'd explain, "MS-DOS stands for Microsoft Disk Operating System. This means that this is the software that operates your disk or your computer."

Someone always asked, "What is Microsoft?"

I would always respond, "It's just the name of the company that made the software. It's some small company. That part doesn't matter." Little did anyone know the future of that small, unknown company!

I am telling you this background because I want to make it clear that I am a pro-technology person. After you hear my personal opinion, you might think that I am an anti-technology person, but that is not the case. People often believe that when you don't like something or you don't support something, it is because you fear it or don't understand it. I do not fear technology, and I think I can safely claim that I understand it much better than most. I sail online wisely and safely, using my MVPs.

My Opinion

This is just my opinion, based on my MVPs. It is not advice, it is not gospel, and it may not be appropriate for your family.

Chat Rooms

I see no reason for children to be in chat rooms. The ethical reasons alone are strong, but the safety risks far outweigh any benefit a child can have from being in a chat room. I have never been in a chat room. I can confidently say that I have not lost out on any opportunities or necessary life skills or knowledge.

Instant Messaging

I see no valid reason for young children to have IM. "Everyone has it" is not a sound or sufficient reason. The ability to hide behind the wall and the mindset that develops from it carry no justification. What is the value in having a cyber social life? Having been on IM myself, I have found myself saying things that I would not ordinarily say face-to-face. I stopped that behavior and placed rules and limitations on myself. I only use it very occasionally.

As a teacher, I am not blind to the tremendous peer pressure that teenagers feel. I, therefore, would find a balance to help relieve some of that pressure. My scale, however, only balances with a small amount of IM allowance on one side and a large amount of real life on the other side. This means that I may allow a high school student to have limited and supervised IM interaction. Because middle school adolescence is all about hormones, feelings, attitudes, and growth, there is too much room, in my opinion, for emotional and ethical damage during these vulnerable years.

Email

I use email, but not as an escape from using the phone. This is a key point, for children need to learn how to speak fluidly while on the phone. Allowing email to take the place of good telephone conversational skills could be a disservice to your child, especially now when the demand for verbal conversational skills is increasing.

I think children can have email. However I agree with Mrs. Smith. I think all email should come through the parents' address for several reasons:

~ It reminds children that all that is written should be viewable by adults. This helps to prevent hiding behind a virtual wall. It also helps to prevent the innocent misunderstandings that occur with the lack of voice intonation, facial expression, and body language. Hopefully, it may deter children from using email too much.

~ It helps protect children from SPAM[23] that might include inappropriate material.

~ It helps protect children from receiving email from strangers, predators, or pedophiles.

As with Mrs. Smith, it does not mean that parents have to read all the email that goes to and from a child's account.

Internet Filtering Software

Absolutely! Why send children out into turbulent, unknown waters without a safety device? With two-thirds of revenue being sex-related, what type of impact would constant exposure to inappropriate sites have on a developing mind of a child, at any age? Peter (from the Jones family story) made the comment that the appearance of pornographic sites happens frequently. How is that chipping away at our society's ethics?

---

[23] SPAM stands for Self-Promoting Advertising Materials. It is basically the online junk mail that includes advertising from all realms, including pornographic solicitations. SPAM is a significant problem that is currently being addressed by legislation.

It seems almost unfair to expect a child to always click on "No" to the "Over 18?" question that prevents them from accessing adult sites. Why give them all this temptation and opportunity for curiosity just to expect them to walk away and ignore it? How would that be different from placing hundreds of adult magazines all over the house and asking them not to touch or look at the magazines? Further, what moral lesson are they learning when they can easily lie about their age with almost no chance of getting caught?

I believe the benefits of filtering software far outweigh the risks of not having it. If it filters out truly needed websites, then parents can always make the adjustment. It's not about trust. It's not about technology. It is about your family.

How Much Time Online?

As little time as possible! Allow your child to be online, but allow just enough time to accomplish what is truly needed. Do homework online. Do research online. Do a quick email here and there. Do family time together online. After that, go outside and play. Play sports. Play an instrument. Draw, read, write. Chat on the phone some. Join groups or clubs. Be a Girl or Boy Scout. Go do some good for their neighborhood, city, country, or world. Find their passion and develop it. Allow your child to develop the skills needed at the crucial human developmental ages. Give your child plenty of opportunity to develop the social skills needed to be a successful adult.

You may be led to believe that as technology replaces some human tasks, the need for social interaction skills will decrease. You may be led to believe that with the use of email and other technology communication, "live" communication skills are a dying breed. The irony behind the technology surge in business and industry today is that the use of technology is actually creating a demand for better personal skills.

For example, many businesses use technology for customer service. The phone system with its, "Press 1 for . . . press 2 for . . ." is one example of this irony. Because of technology, businesses are handling greater volumes of customers and products, therefore using the "press 1, press 2" system. How many times do you wish you could talk to a real person? Many customers are frustrated by it. Therefore, the determining factor in their choice of business today is customer service. Consumers want the face-to-face interaction, the friendly smile, the kind voice, and the personal attention. The more the technology industry presses forward, the more your child will need those "live" social skills to succeed as an adult.[24] Give your child the opportunity to master those skills.

I never touched a computer until I was twenty-two years old. This means I never touched a computer even through my undergraduate college years. My mother started using technology when she was in her fifties and is quite proficient. There is no critical technology learning age. This does not mean that you should keep your child off the computer. Do let your child learn computer technology. Let her learn how to use word processing, spreadsheets, presentation packages, and other "offline" packages. Let her sail the internet safely and ethically with you. Once children learn the basics of technology, they can easily learn any new package. Let your child learn and use technology enough to keep her afloat but not enough to drown her.

Remember, the whole principle is that this is about family and life and not technology. As you move forward, keep in mind the story of the athlete who complains during a tough practice session about how hard it is to be a good athlete. The coach responds, "If it was easy, everyone would do it." Sitting behind a computer is easier than getting up and doing something physical. Which is more rewarding? Which brings more benefits? Why take the easy way out? Being online is easy, so everyone is doing it. Your child is not just everyone. Your child is someone special.

---

[24] This concept is also supported in the Educational Training Service Leadership 2003 Series, which concludes that the new face of the workforce economy requires such skills as listening and oral communication, group interaction, effective teamwork, interpersonal skills, and negotiation. Resource: *Standards for What? The Economic Roots of K-16 Reform,* Anthony P. Carnevale and Donna M. Desrochers, Educational Testing Service, Princeton, NJ, 2003.

Also online: <http://www.ets.org/research/dload/standards_for_what.pdf>

Chapter 9 – Three True Stories

Do you see my three step process here?

1. I put all the information together.

2. I made a balanced decision. I am not saying, "No" to computer time. I am not saying, "No" to online time. I am saying, "Balance the decision." Allow technology, but also allow real life.

3. I sail through the online world. I use my MVPs. I slipped away from them when I was on IM; I slipped away from them when I was on vacation. But I put my MVP sails right back up.

Now, you do the same. The next Chapter has a suggested template for you to use. Use all of it, part of it, or none of it. But do write down a plan. Writing it down gives you even more power.

Closing Comments

Although I may be a bit of a techno geek, I do have other areas in my life. I have my family and friends. I have many interests and hobbies that involve real, face-to-face interactions. Most importantly, I work on my passion:

> *To help parents feel less fearful of the internet and more secure about their decision making, in order to reduce the susceptibility of children being victimized by internet crime or being lured into criminal activity. I cannot stop all online crime, but I can do my part to help maintain the ethical integrity of our society.*

I have been greatly gratified in hearing follow-up stories from families who have attended my seminars or read my articles. It is my sincerest hope that this book had an impact on you. It may be just a small whisper in your ear that might nag at you just enough to put a little more thought into this subject matter. It may lead you to make a positive change for your family.

CHAPTER 10
Your Family's Plan

You are ready to create a customized plan for your family. This plan will be the foundational, non-technical basis that will help you guide your child's online activity. It is just a suggested template. Use part of it or all of it, or create your own. Write directly in this book or rewrite it on a sheet of paper. Do what works best for you. Remember, this is a process. It might need tweaking or modifications in the future, especially as your child ages and as technology changes. Do not expect to make the perfect plan the first go-around. Do not put it off until tomorrow. Do it now. Make a difference for your family and for society.

This book and this non-technical plan were created to get more families involved in their children's online life sooner rather than later. There are many great books and resources that give the technical "How To's," but up to now, many families have not found the time (or the courage, in some cases) to face the intimidating technology. Adopting this family-oriented foundation for your child's online life is easier, faster, and less intimidating. It is also a strong first step toward helping your child and society as a whole.

Hopefully, once you have this solid foundation built, you will be ready to move on to the "How To's" of technology. How do I select the best filtering software? How do I use it? How do I set up a parental control for email?

The Template for Your Plan on pages 78-82 may be copied for personal, home use only. Any other use requires written permission from the Publisher.

Chapter 10 - Your Family's Plan

Template for Your Plan

Suggestions are offered to "get your juices flowing." Work with your child, be creative, and come up with your own ideas as well.

I. Title: Name Your Plan

Suggestions: Sailing the Net with My MVPs
Balanced Decisions Based on My MVPs
For the MVPs of My Life
The Smiths' Computer Plan

Title: _____

II. Goals: Write Your Goals

Suggestions: Maintain the ethical integrity of my family
Develop strong ethics in my child
Maintain or develop strong ethics in my society

Goals:_____

_____

_____

III. MVPs: List Your MVPs

Suggestions: No suggestions here because they have to be your own family's morals, values, and principles.

MVPs:_____

_____

_____

Chapter 10 - Your Family's Plan

IV. The Three Steps: Begin the Process

Step 1: Pull the information together

Indicate which of these pieces of information matter the most to you by copying them or placing a check mark next to them. This is the information on which you will base your decisions.

___ Our society's morals and ethics are slowly transforming.

___ ICE is ice cold. It is a cold method of communication. It does not allow for eye contact, facial expression, body language, or voice intonation. It does allow for frequent misinterpretation and misunderstanding.

___ The exponential growth rate of the internet is unprecedented. This helps to explain the overwhelming feeling of anxiety and fear of the internet.

___ There is no FDA, FCC, Coast Guard, or governing agency for the internet.

___ You do not need to be an internet expert.

___ It is empowering to know that you already have the knowledge and tools that you need to make such a significant, positive impact on your child and on society.

___ Know the Source! Know that the technology industry is the driving force behind the "need" for technology. Human development, research, educational learning, or psychology are not dictating the need for technology use.

___ There is no critical technology learning age. There are critical human development and learning stages.

___ The question is about your family, not technology.

___ How much of a guinea pig are you willing to allow your child to be?

Chapter 10 - Your Family's Plan

__ It is not about trust.

__ The internet is an anyone/anytime/anywhere environment.

__ The internet is still a relatively new worldwide ocean of turbulent waters. You are the primary life-saving device for an invention that has no history or precedent.

__ Laws for your child's safety and protection are still under debate, which emphasizes the essential role of parents.

__ The worldwide web has given your child access to the world, but it has also given the world access to your child.

__ Other:
_____

Step II: Make balanced decisions

1. The ideal age for my child to be on the computer is _____ because

2. The ideal age for my child to be online is _____ because

3. The amount of time my child should be on the computer or online is

    _____ per _____.
    (day/week)

Chapter 10 - Your Family's Plan

4. Activities that are allowed are (homework, research, fun, games, learning, offline software, etc.)

   Suggestion: Ask your child to list the activities she would like to do online and come up with a list on which you both agree.

5. Filtering software <u>will / will not</u> be used because
   circle one

6. Parental control <u>will / will not</u> be used with email because
   circle one

7. The following online activities will be allowed at these ages:

	Email	IM	Chat room	Sail with parent in the room	Sail without parent in the room
Age					

Chapter 10 - Your Family's Plan

8. When my child resists or argues, my standard "mantra" response will be

    Suggestions: Use your goals from the top of this chapter as your responses.
    Use your love for your child as your response.
    Use "because I am the parent" as your response.
    Use whatever falls in line with your MVPs as your response.

    Response: _____

    _____

9. Other activities I will suggest my child be involved with instead of "in front of" time are

    Suggestion: Ask your child!

Step 3: Sail the net with your MVPs

Make a safety and ethics list or have your child create them. Go over each point with your child. Go over this outline with your child. A sample of some safety and ethics points can be found in the Additional Information section.

V. Closing

A. Sign and date your plan.

B. A face-to-face exercise: In PTA groups or any social gathering, ask people to share stories about cyber ethics, crime, or safety. In almost every group, the majority of people will have experienced it themselves or have heard of a story from a friend or the media. Almost everyone has received a virus in an email (although they may not even know it). This is a great learning experience for you. It will open your eyes more and more to the realities of the online world. It may cause you to modify your plan.

C. Think about your next steps. Approach the "technical" side in small steps. For example, your first small step could be to peruse a few of the websites cited in the List of Resources with your child.

Additional Information

Cultivating Criminals?

~

Rules for Safety and Ethics

~

List of Resources

ADDITIONAL INFORMATION
Cultivating Criminals?

To say that you could be cultivating a criminal may sound a bit strong. But is it? Parents, right now, could be unknowingly cultivating future criminals. It may be hard to believe, and your first response may be, "Not my child." No one plans for their child to be criminal, but it is happening. Here is some supporting evidence.

Types of Crimes

The National White Collar Crime Center estimates that one in every three homes is victimized by online crime. Here is a list of some online crimes and methods of crime.

- ~ fraud
- ~ encryption/steganography
- ~ back door techniques
- ~ keystroke monitoring
- ~ denial of service
- ~ trojan horses
- ~ sniffers, sabotage, malicious coding
- ~ viruses
- ~ illegal copying and viewing of data and software
- ~ identity theft
- ~ theft of proprietary information and intellectual property
- ~ stealing of passwords and credit card numbers
- ~ cyberstalking
- ~ crime against children

Tools to commit online crime are often free or inexpensive. For example, it is believed that steganography was a method used in planning terrorist attacks. There are many free steganography software offers online. It is not difficult to learn or use. Another inexpensive tool is keystroke monitoring (as low as $99). On the one hand, it can be a tool for parents to monitor a child's online activity. On the other hand, it can be a tool for criminals to steal passwords and other typed information. Technology like steganography and keystroke monitoring is developed for good purposes but is easily used for criminal activity. Since these tools are free or inexpensive, easy to use, and hard to detect, they create an easily accessible breeding ground for crime.

Types of Criminals

When you hear about online crimes in the media, you often hear about foreign governments, economic espionage, corporate competitors, and terrorists. You may think that it is just the few bad apples that commit online crimes. But the reality is that 80% of cyber attacks do not come from the criminals listed above. They are committed by the everyday adult, who has become disgruntled or unhappy with an employer, partner, or some type of work affiliation. This means that the normally good citizen, who would never even steal a candy bar, is committing online crimes that cost millions and can hurt many.

But it is not just adults who commit online crimes. Many cases involve children as well. For example:

> A 16-year-old committed a serious crime to a high-level government office, stealing passwords, entering secure areas, and accessing files. When caught, his response was, *"It had just been a game or a challenge from which I had got a real buzz . . . I never thought I would get caught, and it was very disturbing when I did."*[25]

Think about the statement that he was very **disturbed** when he got caught. Why? Were his actions just an online game and he did not understand the reality of it? Did he think there was no one on the other end?

---

[25] Crime story resource: <http://www.cybercrime.gov>, which is the website for the Computer Crime and Intellectual Property Section of the Criminal Division of the U.S. Department of Justice. The website lists recently prosecuted cases by the Department of Justice.

Additional Information – Cultivating Criminals?

Here are some other stories of online crime which involved children.

~ A juvenile in Massachusetts pleaded guilty to charges of disabling a network which affected an airport control tower as well as the signals that activated the runway lights.

~ A 16-year-old from Florida pleaded guilty and was sentenced for intercepting electronic communications on military computer networks and for illegally obtaining information from a NASA computer network.

~ A 16-year-old in Virginia pleaded guilty to computer trespassing after hacking into an ISP's computer system, causing $20,000 in damages.

~ A 13-year-old California boy pleaded guilty to making threats directed against a 13-year-old girl over the internet. The website included a petition calling for the girl's death.

~ Stock manipulation fraud caused an $800,000 loss.

In many instances, the charged criminal denied serious intentions, but was rather trying to impress peers or was just playing a challenging game. Is this because they do not fully understand that it is reality? Do they not realize that their typing on the keyboard has a true effect on "the receiving side"? Is it because they do not see their victims? Is it because they do not understand the magnitude of their actions? How does that mentality all start? Could it start with ICE?

The Buck Doesn't Stop Here

When reading those headline stories, people may think those crimes were unusual instances or that only the one-in-a-million child would commit such a serious crime. Again, it is not just the "bad kids" who are committing online crimes. One of the biggest problems with students and online crime is committed by children from all neighborhoods, all types of families, and even from the best schools: copyright infringement. Although breaking the copyright law may not seem as serious as hacking the Pentagon's network, copyright infringement is a crime punishable by law and can be as serious as a felony. Due to the rampant nature of copyright violations, a greater effort is being made not only to control the ability to make illegal copies, but also to track and prosecute violators.

Breach of copyright law includes many areas such as copying software, using pictures, cutting and pasting text, and the media saturated topic of downloading and copying music. Take a look at just two of these areas.

Music Piracy

There is enormous amount of illegal downloading of music. Law suits and cases are abundant in the headlines. According to a survey,

> "88 percent of kids between the ages of 8 and 18 know that most popular music is copyrighted, but 56 percent download music files anyway. Survey participants said they were generally more concerned about downloading viruses in music files than being prosecuted for copyright violations."[26]

What does it mean that children are more concerned about "catching a virus" than breaking the law?

Plagiarism

The other widespread area of crime is plagiarism. With the abundant amount of information available online, students are presented with great temptation to plagiarize. In a survey at the University of Virginia, faculty cited the internet as the number one reason students commit acts

---

[26] *Survey Finds U.S. Kids Continue Downloads,* Educause listserv newsletter, June 2004. This story is a summary of a Washington Post article published May 18, 2004, http://www.washingtonpost.com/wp-dyn/articles/A37231-2004May18.html. Realize that only 56% admitted to it. Could the percentage be much higher? For more information about the issue with music piracy, see the Recording Industry Association of America's website: http://www.riaa.com/default.asp.

of plagiarism. In another survey of 4,500 students at twenty-five high schools, over half of the students admitted they engaged in some level of plagiarism on written assignments using the internet. Internet plagiarism is so abundant that software has been developed for teachers to use that can detect if students have copied information from online sources. Students have rebelled against teachers using this software, claiming that it is a violation of their trust. Are you starting to see a recurring theme?

The problem is a significant national issue which resulted in the No Electronic Theft Act. With the birth of the internet, the Copyright Act was not comprehensive enough to cover online issues. Therefore, the new act was developed to cover online copyright infringements. It

> *"now allows criminal prosecution of online copyright infringement, even by people sharing copyrighted software or games online . . . in particular the infringement by teenagers."* [27]

Note the last six words.[28]

What does this all mean? How is today's stealing music online any different from yesterday's stealing a *vinyl record album* from the store? Are our children committing these crimes because they are in the comfort of their homes, just typing on a keyboard? Do they understand the reality of what they are doing? Is it not "real" because they do not see anyone, feel anyone's reaction, or grasp the concept that they are stealing from and harming others? Does the "it's not real" mindset then breed and multiply upon itself, resulting in online hacking, theft, trespassing, and other felonies?

---

[27] Copyright link on http://www.cyberangels.org/law/copyrights/index.html. Guardian Angels / CyberAngels, no date cited. (Accessed in 2001.) To see a summary of the law: http://www.usdoj.gov/criminal/cybercrime/netsum.htm/.

[28] To help your child better understand copyright regulations, consult your child's school, as the school may have a concise list of copyright rules as they pertain to education. You can also call the U.S. Copyright Office (202) 707-3000 or access it online at http://www.copyright.gov.

The Recurring Theme

In reviewing these surveys, articles, and crime cases about our children, you can see a shift in the ethical understanding in today's children who are growing up in a whole new environment, the online world.

~ A 16-year-old finds it disturbing that he was caught. Is it not disturbing he found it disturbing?

~ Teens committed federal crimes to impress their peers or because it was a challenging game. Did they even consider the seriousness of their actions or the damaging effects?

~ Many students are (anonymously) admitting to online plagiarism. Yet, students feel that plagiarism-catching software is a violation of their trust. Is there a conflict here?

~ A new copyright law had to be enacted particularly for "the infringement by teenagers." Are teenagers now more prone to breaking the law?

The 16-year-old in the first example probably would not have physically climbed the walls of the government building, broken into a locked room, picked the lock on the filing cabinet, and stolen passwords. Even children probably realize that would be a flagrant crime. Yet that is basically what he had done, except he did it online, and just to get a buzz. People, hiding behind a virtual wall, unable to see the damages they have done, are not understanding that there is no difference between an online crime and a physical crime. In reality, an online crime can be much worse and can cause much more damage.

Online Crime is Not an Exception to the Rule

Online crime does not just happen in the bad neighborhoods. It is not committed by just the "bad guys." It is not an exception to the rule. Online crime occurs everywhere, in every neighborhood. It does not discriminate against color, race, or gender. It accounts for billions of dollars of loss revenue. No one can accurately estimate the loss because many companies and individuals do not report losses. Also, the internet is worldwide, making it even more difficult to accurately track the financial, personal, or human loss caused by online crime. Every person online is susceptible to being a criminal or a victim.

In case you are still not quite convinced, think about the headline news ten years ago. Compare it to just a few recent headlines in the news today[29] (from Spring/Summer 2004). Some of these words (e.g. phishing) were not even in your vocabulary ten years ago. You might not even be familiar with them today, but they are making the headlines.

    FTC Requires Labels for Porn Spam
    Gartner Estimates U.S. Lost $2.4 Billion in 2003 to Online Fraud
    New Group Forming to Fight Online Identity Fraud
    Phishing Scams Grow in Number and Sophistication
    Survey Finds U.S. Kids Continue (Illegal) Downloads
    That E-Mail from the Network Administrator Could be a Virus
    Copyright Apathy on the Rise
    Study Links Internet Overuse with Depression
    Cyberstalker Pleads Guilty
    Worm Variant Clogs E-Mail, Search Engines
    Web Sites Hacked and Code Put on Servers
    E-Mail Addresses Sold to Spammers
    Student Hackers in Hot Water at Oxford
    Report Shows Steep Rise in Software Piracy

Summary

These are only a few examples. Online crime is not the exception. It is a worldwide reality growing in immeasurable proportions. As users of the internet, you and your child are subject to both the criminal and the victim aspects.

---

[29] These headlines came from Edupage. *Edupage* is an email listserv that summarizes developments in information technology. Edupage copyright 2004, EDUCAUSE. http://www.educause.edu/pub/edupage/.

Therefore, both issues need to be addressed. Which do we address first, the chicken or the egg? Do we try to prevent cultivating criminals so that there will be no more victims? In the meantime, the problem does exist, and you are susceptible to being a victim. Do we focus on your safety first? In the meantime, we are cultivating criminals. The answer, of course, is both. Do both.

Therefore this series of books will do exactly that. This first book is building the foundation for both and focusing on the ethical considerations. It is developed first because the foundational skills in this book will naturally lead to keeping your family safe. The next book will take the foundation set here and apply it toward the safety issue. In the meantime, of course, there are many resources for you, as listed in the List of Resources section.

Although this book cannot prevent the cultivation and harvesting of every online criminal, perhaps it can help the cause, one family at a time.

ADDITIONAL INFORMATION
Rules for Safety and Ethics

Every family should have rules or guidelines for their children's online activity. You can have one set of rules that covers both the ethical and safety issues, or you can have two separate sets of rules, one about ethics and the other about safety. It does not matter if your family writes one or two sets of rules. It only matters that you have rules.

To help you get started, the next several pages contain common rules for online ethical behavior (*Netiquette*) and common rules for safety. Use some of them or all of them, or create some of your own. But do have a set of rules or guidelines for your child.

> This process could take as little as five minutes. Spend five minutes to help protect your child's safety and ethical integrity.

The Five-Minute Approach

Sit down with your child and go through the next several pages. Put a check mark next to those rules that will apply to your family. Sign and date the bottom of each section. Have your child lead a brief discussion with you as to why each checked item was chosen.

A Customized Approach

Customize and create a set of rules for your family. You can keep this simple or make it into a fun family project. For example, the rules can be simply written or typed. For a project, have your child design the document, add pictures, use color, make a cover, or include any fun personal touch. However you choose to approach it, do write it down. Use any or all of the suggested steps.

Suggested Steps for Customizing Rules for Your Family

1. Go through the next several pages and place a check next to the rules you will use.

2. Add any of your own rules to the list.

3. If necessary, rewrite the rules into your own words to best fit your family.

4. Create a title for your rules. Use a standard title or be creative.
    "Because I Love You" Rules
    Sailing the Seas with Sense
    Wise Words for the Web

5. Have your child write or type your customized list of rules.

6. Have your child lead a discussion about each rule and its purpose.

7. Parents and children should sign and date the rules.

8. Write down a review schedule. For example: Review every two weeks or review once a month. The rules should be reviewed occasionally to see if they need to be changed, updated, or even deleted. Write the review schedule on your calendar, daytimer, or refrigerator. Review the rules sooner than the scheduled time, if necessary.

9. Decide with your child on the best location to place the rules.

10. Sail the Net with Your MVPs!

Additional Information – Rules for Safety and Ethics

Netiquette Rules

These two pages regarding Netiquette Rules may be copied for personal, home use only. Any other use requires written permission from the Publisher.

These are some of the commonly suggested tips for etiquette (ethical behavior) on the net, which is sometimes called *Netiquette*. For other rules or more details, refer to the List of Resources.

___ I will apply the Golden Rule to my online activity: Do unto others as you would have others do unto you.

___ I will only type what I would say to a person face-to-face.

___ I know that sarcasm and humor cannot be "read" and messages can be misunderstood, even with the use of emoticons. I will try not to write messages that could be misunderstood.

___ If I receive an unkind, offensive, or inappropriate message, I will not respond to it. If I feel the need to respond, I will ask a parent for guidance.

___ I will not use the internet or ICE to escape live, social interaction with my friends.

___ I will not give out my passwords or login/screen names, and I will not ask other people for their passwords or personal information.

___ I will always respect everyone's privacy online.

___ I will never use the computer to snoop, steal, or break into anyone's information.

___ I will obey and respect all copyright laws. Copying any pictures, text, ideas, software, or music online could be illegal, even if "everyone is doing it." Before I copy or download anything from the internet, I need to find out from a teacher or an adult if I am legally allowed to do so.

Additional Information – Rules for Safety and Ethics

—   I need to remember that not everything that is written online is necessarily right or true. I need to remember that not everyone is who they claim to be online.

—   I will respect the filtering software that has been installed on the computer.

—   If I do hit an inappropriate site, I will close it immediately and inform a parent.

—   I will respect the time and location rules of usage set by my family . . . (Write your personal guidelines):

Child(ren)
Signature(s): _____

_____

Parent(s)
Signature(s):_____

_____

Date: _____

To be reviewed every: _____

Additional Information – Rules for Safety and Ethics

Safety Rules

These two pages regarding Safety Rules may be copied for personal, home use only. Any other use requires written permission from the Publisher.

These are just some of the commonly suggested tips for safe sailing. There are other rules and some that go into greater detail. For other rules or more details, refer to the List of Resources.

__ I will not respond to messages that make me feel uncomfortable, seem improper, or appear threatening. I will not respond to any messages that use bad language. I will tell a parent right away.

__ I will not give my passwords or login/screen names to anyone.

__ I will never give **any** personal information on the web or if using ICE, including:

   my name or any family member's name
   my address or phone number
   my age, where I go to school, or my picture
   credit card numbers, calling card numbers, or any numbers

__ I will be careful about anything I type online because nothing I write on the web is completely private -- including email.

__ I will not meet or make plans to meet with anyone I have met on the internet without the presence and knowledge of a parent.

__ I will not buy anything online without a parent's knowledge and consent.

__ I will not accept gifts from strangers.

__ I will not "talk" to strangers online. Not everyone is who they say they are.

Additional Information – Rules for Safety and Ethics

— I will not download or open any attachments from unknown sources.

— My family will keep the computer in the _____, which is an open family area.

— When in doubt, log out!

— Per my family's rules, I will only sail on the net . . . (Write your personal guidelines):

Child(ren)
Signature(s): _____

_____

Parent(s)
Signature(s):_____

_____

Date: _____

To be reviewed every: _____

ADDITIONAL INFORMATION
List of Resources

This section lists:

1. References used for research for this book that were not included in footnote notations.

2. Further resources for your use and information.

About the websites:

There are many websites listed. For readers who are not comfortable with sailing the web yet (and even those who are), use this opportunity to:

1. Spend time with your child online.

2. Have your child teach you the "new stuff" (technology) while you teach her the "old stuff" (family values and ethics). This provides her a sense of pride (being the teacher), responsibility (teaching), and valuable family time.

3. Learn!

You can also call the main sponsor of a webpage and ask for pamphlets or other hard-copy information that might be available.

Additional Information – List of Resources

During the research process, all websites listed in footnotes and in this section were active and accessible. If you are unable to access a website:

1. Check to make sure you typed every character in correctly. Each character must be exact.

2. Try again later. The website may be temporarily offline.

3. The website may no longer exist. Not all websites stay online indefinitely. If you have tried the website on several different occasions and it does not work, it is probably no longer active.

Safety & Ethics

Department of Education: Internet Safety Issues
http://www.ed.gov/about/offices/list/os/technology/safety.html
Telephone: 1-877-4-ED-PUBS

The FBI's publication: A Parent's Guide to Internet Safety
http://www.fbi.gov/publications/pguide/pguidee.htm
Telephone: (202) 324-3666

Department of Justice: Cyberethics for Kids
http://www.cybercrime.gov/rules/kidinternet.htm
Telephone: (202) 514-1026

There are many websites which cover the safety issue. These are just a few suggested websites. Use references and resources from other colleagues as well.

- ~ http://www.cyberangels.org
- ~ http://www.cybercitizenship.org/crime/safety.html
- ~ http://www.getnetwise.org
- ~ http://www.isafe.org

Additional Information – List of Resources

Computer Crime

<u>US Department of Justice</u>
Computer Crime and Intellectual Property Section
http://www.cybercrime.gov
Cyberstalking
http://www.usdoj.gov/criminal/cybercrime/cyberstalking.htm

<u>National White Collar Crime Center</u>
http://www.nw3c.org/

<u>Department of Energy</u>
List of rumors and hoaxes on email viruses
http://hoaxbusters.ciac.org/

<u>FBI</u>
Internet Fraud Complaint Center
http://www.ifccfbi.gov/
Online child pornography: http://www.fbi.gov/hq/cid/cac/innocent.htm
Kidnapping: http://www.fbi.gov/hq/cid/cac/kidnap.htm

Contact your local FBI field office
http://www.fbi.gov/contact/fo/fo.htm
Scroll down to find your local office by city or state.

<u>Reporting Cybercrime</u>
How to Report Internet-Related Crime
http://www.usdoj.gov/criminal/cybercrime/reporting.htm

Report to Cybertipline http://www.cybertipline.com

National Child Pornography Tipline 800-843-5678 (800-THE-LOST)

Additional Information – List of Resources

Books

Failure to Connect: How Computers Affect Our Children's Minds—and What We Can Do About It. Jane M. Healy, Touchstone, 1998.

The books listed here were used as general resources. Contact your local bookstore for other options or use online sources such as:

~ http://www.amazon.com
~ http://www.borders.com
~ http://www.barnesandnoble.com

The Parent's Guide to Protecting Your Children in Cyberspace. Parry Aftab, McGraw-Hill, 2000.

Kids Online: Protecting Your Children in Cyberspace. Donna Rice Hughes, Fleming H. Revell, 1998.

Other Resources

http://kids.getnetwise.org/tools/index.php -- on filtering software GetNetWise, © 1999-2003 Internet Education Foundation.

http://www.infowar.com/iwftp/icn/04Sep2001_Cheating's_Never_Been_Easier.shtml
Info.com, ©2003 Interpact, Inc.

http://abcnews.go.com/sections/tech/DailyNews/nasa000712.html
ABC News, ©2004 ABCNEWS Internet Ventures.

http://www.infowar.com/hacker/01/hack_011201c_j.shtml
Info.com, ©2003 Interpact, Inc.

http://www.infowar.com/hacker/hack_040498d_j.html-ssi
Info.com, ©2003 Interpact, Inc.

Additional Information – List of Resources

http://www.ssrn.com/update/lsn/cyberspace/csl_lessons.html
Social Science Research Network, ©2004 Social Science Electronic Publishing, Inc.

http://www.spa.org/piracy/default.asp
Software Information Industry Association, ©2004 The Software & Information Industry Association.

http://www.fau.edu/netiquette/net/ten.html
Florida Atlantic University, ©1998 Arlene Rinaldi & Florida Atlantic University.

http://www.chowan.edu/acadp/computer/netetiquette/corerules.html
Chowan College ©1994-97 Albion.com.

http://www.cio.com/research/behavior/
Cyber Behavior Research Center ©1994 - 2004 CXO Media Inc.

http://www.csc.calpoly.edu/~ebrunner/CyberEthicChart.html
California Polytechnic State University, Department of Computer Science, Cyber Ethics: Legal & Moral Issues on the Web, Prepared by Elizabeth Brunner.

http://www.copyright.gov
The Library of Congress, U.S. Copyright Office, July 2004.
Phone: (202) 707-3000

http://www.whatiscopyright.org/
WhatisCopyright.org © 1998-2003 WhatisCopyright.org.

Seminar information from 5th National Colloquium for Information Systems Security Education, May 2001 at George Mason University, Virginia.

Seminar information from National Cyber Ethics Conference, October 2000 at Marymount University, Virginia.

Printed in the United States
26083LVS00006B/283-402